You and Your Ascendant

Sophia Mason

Copyright 1998 by Sophia Mason
All rights reserved.

No part of this book may be reproduced or transmitted in any form or by any means, electronic or mechanical, including photocopying or recording, or by any information storage and retrieval system, without written permission from the author and publisher. Requests and inquiries may be mailed to: American Federation of Astrologers, Inc., PO Box 22040, Tempe, AZ 85284-2040.

ISBN: 0-86690-488-3

Current Printing: 1998

Illustrations by Howard Duff, reprinted with permission

Published by:
American Federation of Astrologers, Inc.
PO Box 22040
6535 S. Rural Road
Tempe, AZ 85285-2040

Printed in the United States of America

Contents

Introduction	1
Natal Chart	5
Aries Ascendant	13
Taurus Ascendant	23
Gemini Ascendant	35
Cancer Ascendant	47
Leo Ascendant	59
Virgo Ascendant	73
Libra Ascendant	87
Scorpio Ascendant	103
Sagittarius Ascendant	117
Capricorn Ascendant	133
Aquarius Ascendant	149
Pisces Ascendant	161

Introduction

No matter what zodiac sign is on the Ascendant, unless they are twins no two individuals will resemble each other exactly. The configurations listed below are the main factors that will alter one's appearance and temperament, and indicate what interests may play an important role in the native's life.

First and foremost are planets conjunct the Ascendant within a five degree orb. It matters not whether the planet is in the twelfth or first house, however planets in the first will have an external influence upon the individual, while planets conjunct the Ascendant from the twelfth will operate internally, on the emotional level.

Planets aspecting the Ascendant, but not conjunct it, are the next consideration. A seven degree orb is usually given for the Sun and Moon, and a five degree orb for the rest of the planets.

Planets in the first house that do not conjunct the Ascendant will also color the native according to the planet's energy and sign containment.

The house position of the Ascendant ruler indicates the area of life that influences the individual from time to time. The sign position of the ruler indicates the motivational influences through which the individual utilizes the house position of the ruler. The aspects to the ruler indicate the type of energy one exerts to influence the conditioning of the house and sign placement.

Next in importance are the house, sign and aspects to the Sun. The sign position of the Sun indicates the internal influence that goes into planning a project or thought matter.

The Moon is of equal importance to the Sun. Its position by house, sign and aspect indicates the external influences through which one takes action upon the project or thought matter that concerned the Sun.

According to sign position, both the Sun and Moon add a touch of their features to the native's appearance.

Planets that are exact or within one degree orb of conjunction always have a personal effect upon the native according to the house and sign position.

This does not imply that planets in the uppermost part of the chart are to be ignored. These are merely indicators that are likely to color the character traits and temperament of the individual according to aspects to the Ascendant's degree and ruler, as well as the Sun and Moon.

The following features are always given serious consideration as they play an important role in the native's life according to the house and sign placement. Although they may not alter the body structure or temperament, they will have an external role in the individual's life and experiences. They will be covered in more depth later in this book.

The planet most elevated in the natal chart will, at some point in life, have a marked influence upon the native. To determine which planet is the most elevated (if there are planets in the ninth and tenth houses), subtract the degrees from the tenth house cusp to find the one closest to the Midheaven.

A singleton planet, no matter where it is placed in the chart, is also given serious consideration. A singleton planet is one that is by itself, with the closest aspect on either side being a sextile. It has more determination for good or evil because its course of action is not as quickly changed, unlike the individual with a scattering of planets and no singleton. As transiting planets head toward the singleton, it takes them longer to get there and just as long to leave. One has more time to develop a personal interest or goal in life, and there is more determination to succeed or, if handled incorrectly, to fail.

Planets in close aspect with one another, preferably exact or within one degree orb, play a major role in the native's life. Sextiles and trines indicate creative talents in a specialized field. Exact squares, oppositions, semisquares and sesquiquadrates indicate obstacles in life that one has to contend with. In many cases squares build strength of character because adversity teaches perseverance and fortitude.

Planets in angular houses should never be discounted. They are the cardinal houses and indicate ambition to succeed in some particular field according to the planets involved.

Keep in mind that the Sun, Moon, Mercury, Venus and Mars are personal planets. Aspects involving these planets usually react early in life.

The slower moving planets—Jupiter, Saturn, Uranus, Neptune and Pluto—usually affect the character traits later in life, after the twenty-first birthday or when the individual starts to mature. However, if the natal Sun, for example, squares natal Pluto, this will operate during the formative years. Then as the maturation process continues, the individual realizes that an aggressive, domineering attitude is not conducive to a successful career. At that point the native begins to take stock of himself and learns the art of compromise and cooperation.

In this book, each ascending sign is correlated with the planet, sign and house, but the planetary placements need not be confined to the ascending sign. Anyone with planets in a specific sign and house will feel the effect in a fashion similar to the Ascendant's ruler, but perhaps not with the intensity unless the planet is in aspect with the ascending degree or the Ascendant's ruler, or it is the ruler of the Ascendant's decan or dwad.

Do not limit these configurations to the natal chart. They can be used with a separate progressed chart, so note the progressed Ascendant sign, its ruler and house position, as well as any planets in the house and sign.

In the Ascendant sign sections dealing with the houses ruled by the slow-moving planets—Jupiter, Saturn, Uranus, Neptune, Pluto—the information can be applied to the planets in transit. Because they move so slowly, their influences have far-reaching effects.

Natal Chart

The natal chart reveals a good percentage of life's predictions, but it is impossible to determine all aspects of life just from the natal chart. Progressions, the major transits, lunations and eclipses will also draw events, people and circumstances into your life according to the aspects. Therefore, each and every planet in the natal and progressed charts will receive both favorable and unfavorable aspects from transits, lunations and eclipses. This is why life seldom runs on an even keel; there is always one major planet lurking in the bush, waiting to stir up something in a chart. How these events transpire depends on the way the individual reacts to the planetary aspects and configurations.

Planetary Sign Positions

Make it a habit to verify planetary placement when planets are activated by a major transit, lunation or eclipse. Should transiting Uranus in Aquarius, for example, trine natal Venus in Libra, immediately check the condition of the seventh house (Libra), planets therein and the ruler of that house. If nothing is highlighting the seventh house, go to the eleventh house (Uranus in Aquarius) and do likewise, checking planets (natal or transit) therein, the ruler (natal and transit) and the aspects made to them. If neither the seventh nor the eleventh houses offer any clue to the situation at hand, check the houses that Venus and Uranus rule and repeat the process. One aspect will never make a event or describe the condition of it.

Decanates and Dwads

Decanates and dwads are the divisions of zodiacal signs by ten degrees and two and a half degrees.

Dwads are divided by two degrees, thirty minutes, but sometimes it is unclear which dwad the Ascendant falls in. For example, someone born with 7 Taurus 30 could have a Cancer dwad or a Leo dwad, if the birth time is off by a minute or two. Always give consideration to the decanate and dwad rulers because they are close underlying factors and character traits that would otherwise go unnoticed. If this Taurus rising individual were born a minute earlier, he would be excellent in money management, real estate, banking and housing, and be more sensitive to the needs of others having a Cancerian trait. It is possible the individual will inherit property (Cancer dwad) or possessions (Taurus rising) form a parent.

But if the Ascendant is 7 Taurus 30 or if the native was born perhaps one minute later, the dwad is Leo. Much depends upon the aspects to the Sun, ruler of the Leo dwad, but this individual would want to be in a position of money (Taurus) management or in some way be a boss or supervisor. Children (Leo) may have some effect upon personal finances (Taurus rising). The individual would love luxury items or purchase second best if unable to afford the (Leo) best of products. This, however, does convey a stubborn attitude, one who will listen but go his own Leo way. The placement of the natal Sun will play an important role in this native's life and its sign position will instill an additional character trait that would not ordinarily be detected.

One of my clients, a physician, has the Sun in his tenth house at 7 Taurus 32. It is in the Leo dwad and he earns his income (Taurus) as a child specialist (Leo dwad), and at one time delivered babies. This man's dwad is very strong because his Sun in Taurus rules the Leo dwad which adds emphasis to his choice of career. The ruler of his Taurus Sun is Venus and it is placed in the twelfth house in Cancer. That explains that his career (tenth house) has him working in a hospital (ruler Venus in the twelfth house) with mothers (Cancer) and with children.

Anytime the ruler of a sign of house cusp aspects the decanate or dwad ruler, there is always added emphasis and importance placed upon the planet in question. Sixteen degrees of Aries is on my second house cusp. Mars rules that house cusp and is conjoined with Venus, ruler of the dwad. Both Venus and Mars are in Leo in the sixth house. When my son started a new job, he was not yet covered by insurance. He had an accident requiring surgery and a brief hospital stay, yet the bill was more than $3,000. I paid (Mars on the second house cusp governing accidents in the Leo decanate) my son's bill. It was a good thing that my personal finances were assisted by the Libra dwad—my husband (Libra) was earning quite a bit of money at that time and the $3,000 was no hardship. We also paid for all our children's weddings (Sun in Cancer, ruler of the Leo decan, semisquares Venus, ruler of the Aries dwad). The future mothers-in-law of both sons were widows, so we felt obligated.

Intercepted First House

Individuals who have an intercepted sign in their first house are unique. They have two rulers that have to be taken into consideration, the one on the house cusp and the one governing the intercepted sign. These individuals generally have more than one personal project, interest or relationship that will react upon their lives at some time or another. They lead a more active life than the average individual because the transits have two planets they can aspect, which in turn impact the first house.

The sign on the cusp of the first house indicates the general character traits and physical features, but never underestimate the intercepted sign. If, for example, the individual has Pisces on the first house cusp with Aries intercepted in the first house, the person can be a real pushover and easily led or influenced, but only for a short time. When and if the individual feels he has been taken unfair advantage of, he will lash out in an aggressive manner, in anger and heated temper. Then in true Piscean manner, he will write the enemy off and have nothing more to do with him.

Planets in the first house positioned in the intercepted sign take precedence over the sign on the house cusp. These planets may lay dormant, but will surface whenever aspected and override the sign of the first house cusp.

Sometimes individuals with an intercepted first house overcompensate for something that was lacking in their early years and go out of their way to please and appease others.

Note the two planets that rule the sign on the first house cusp and the intercepted sign by house, sign and aspect. Should the ruler of the first house cusp unfavorably aspect the ruler of the intercepted sign in the first, the individual has an inner psychological conflict that may surface in a negative fashion. This aspect may also indicate personal obstacles that must be overcome, either in health, vocation or relationships.

With soft aspects between the two rulers the native overcomes any obstacle that may confront him, but as a rule life runs rather smoothly where personal affairs are concerned. There are no inner psychological problems or quirks in the nature, and these individuals have good common sense and sound judgment which are applied to everyday affairs.

If no aspect occurs between the two rulers, and one is receiving a hard aspect while the other has nothing but soft aspects, then one has to give due consideration to each planet separately. The sign position and area of life (house position) will disclose where one is likely to be confronted by obstacles and where one can expect an easy flow of events or circumstances. These are the houses and sign positions of the two rulers, the one on the house cusp and the one governing the intercepted sign.

Planets in the first house in the sign on the cusp of the second house, but not in the intercepted sign, will have a personal effect upon the individual but are more likely to react upon personal earnings, finances and possessions. Because the planet is in the sign that is on the second house cusp, the native will earn money according to the planet and its sign position.

Art of Synthesis

When one studies a natal chart, it can be a perplexing problem trying to determine where to begin. My first choice is an intercepted house. Why? Because intercepted signs are important and should never be ignored. Interceptions are formed through the curvature of the Earth's surface, which causes a distortion in house sizes depending on the distance north or south of the equator. The farther north or south one is born, the more chance o having a chart containing intercepted signs. People born in latitudes higher than fifty degrees north or south may have more than one sign intercepted in a house. Due to the vast difference in climatic conditions, these individuals live differently from those in more moderate climes.

Houses with intercepted signs are important because they can contain as many as forty-five degrees or even more pr house. Even if the house is unoccupied, it till remains a number one priority. Consider the fact that three planets will influence these houses: the planet that rules the house cusp, the planet that rules the intercepted sign and the planet that rules the sign on the next house. Should either of these two houses contain a planet, then that house will be the focal point of the chart, especially so if the planet therein rules the sign on the house cusp, the intercepted sign, the sign on the next house or if any of these three rulers are in aspect with one another. A great deal of character insight, as well as the life purpose of these individuals, is gained through careful analysis of these two houses.

The intercepted sign remains dormant, so to speak, until the occasion arises that the person must draw upon the motivational influence of that sign. For example, Pisces on the Ascendant can be submissive with an aim-to-please type of personality; however, with Aries intercepted in the first house, he will express his own individual rights with a force of temper if necessary. With Taurus on the second house, he succeeds in any personal endeavor through "constancy of purpose," which others may view as bullheadedness.

If there are no planets in intercepted houses, note the three rulers thereof by house, sign and aspects thereto, and learn to channel the circumstances of their position through the houses they rule. For example, with Aquarius rising, Pisces intercepted and Aries on the second house cusp, if Neptune is in the sixth house and Mars is in the ninth house, then the affairs of work, health and distant matters play a personal role in the life of the native.

With two houses having intercepted signs, there will be two houses with twenty-five degrees or less contained therein. When transits, especially the major transits (Jupiter, Saturn, Uranus, Neptune and Pluto) enter these two short houses, their actions will be swifter with rapid changes because they will not remain too long in that particular house, with only the ruler of the house cusp to consider.

When transits enter an intercepted house, they remain there for longer periods, giving one more time to develop and promote interests concerning matters related to those two houses. Transiting Venus, Mercury and Mars are swift moving plant,s but should they be retrograde in motion while in an intercepted house, they gain as much importance as the major planets. And every time one of these transits—major planets or minor retrogrades—changes signs, one will be motivated into a different direction or course of action or experience new events.

Constitution and Elements

The second step, if there are no intercepted sign, is to consider the constitution and the elements as another important factor in viewing the type of horoscope as a whole. Understanding these two principles can help in determining the individual's general characteristics and mode of action. Some astrologer refer to them as the "basic drive," or "final signature."

Cardinal Signs: Aries, Cancer, Libra, Capricorn. Notice how they are all related to the angular houses, the first, fourth, seventh and tenth. When the majority of planets are in cardinal signs, these people are initiators, ambitious and enterprising.

Each sign initiates in a different way. Aries initiates action for the promotion of personal goals and self-centered interests. Cancer initiates action toward the preservation of inner security, protection of family and home. Libra initiates action toward teamwork, marriage and business partnerships or close associations. Capricorn initiates action that will enhance public image, business and professional interests.

Fixed Signs: Taurus, Leo, Scorpio, Aquarius. Notice how they all govern succedent houses, the second, fifth, eighth and eleventh. Those with the majority of planets in fixed signs are stubborn, determined and goal oriented. However, once a goal has been determined and set into motion, there is a fixity of purpose to see it through to the bitter end. Taurus is goal oriented in connection with personal finances and possessions. However if carried to the extreme, they can become pack-rats, holding onto useless items, magazines or outdated clothing. Leos are goal oriented toward enhancement of their ego and pride, which is why they often prefer luxurious items that reflect upon their status. Their stubborn pride sometimes doe snot want to admit defeat and as a result they often stay with a romantic interest or i a stagnant marriage log after it should have been reasonably discontinued. Scorpios are goal oriented through mutual funding or possessions gained through the resources of others. They should guard against the tendency to go to extremes, becoming obsessive, possessive or dictatorial. Aquarius, on the other hand, is people oriented and likes to know what makes others tick. They have to avoid a stubborn adherence to their own theories and ideas and realize there is room for changing opinions and a willingness to accept them.

Mutable Signs: Gemini, Virgo, Sagittarius, Pisces. Notice how these signs govern the cadent houses, the third, sixth, ninth and twelfth. People with the majority of planets in mutable signs are adaptable and can readily adjust themselves to the needs of others. These individuals are people oriented. Gemini generates toward others through their communication skills. Virgo is people oriented through the services and care they provide others. Sagittarius is people oriented through religion and higher learning. Pisces is people oriented through a sympathetic, supportive and compassionate nature.

The elements are the second grouping of signs which are commonly called the triplicities. They contain four groups of three signs each, which respond to the spirit, body, mind and soul of man.

Fire Signs: Aries, Leo, Sagittarius. Notice how they govern the first, fifth and ninth houses. People with the majority of signs in the fire element are ambitious, assertive and enterprising. These are the go-getter types who have the energy and the enthusiasm to pursue a desired goal, but not always in the practical sense.

Earth Signs: Taurus, Virgo, Capricorn. Notice how they govern the second, sixth and tenth houses. People with the majority of planets in earth elements are dependable and practical. They are stabilizers who assimilate, build, gather and collect with an inclination to be materialistic in the protective sense.

Air Signs: Gemini, Libra, Aquarius. Notice how they govern the third, seventh and eleventh houses. The air element gives geniality and the ability to associate with others freely. They are thinkers, possessing intuitive, inspiration and intellectual skills.

Water Signs: Cancer, Scorpio, Pisces. Notice how they govern the fourth, eighth and twelfth houses. The water element colors the nature with strong emotional sensitivity and psychic or intuitive powers. They are sustainers, offering nurturing support and sympathy when needed.

Stellium

The third step is to look for a stellium of planets—three or more planets in a sign, but they need not be conjucnt. No matter what the Ascendant, Sun or Moon sign, if there are three or more planets in the same sign the character traits of that sign will reveal themselves from time to time and should be given prime consideration in delineation of one's character ad motivational influences. The same principle should be applied with three or more planet in one house, regardless if one of them should happen to be in a different sign position. The character and conditioning of the matters ruled by the house will also manifest themselves. For example, people with no planet is Scorpio but three or more planet sin the eighth house will possess some of the characteristics of Scorpio and be strongly influenced by mutual funds, sexual interests and death, or be obsessed with matters of the hereafter.

Aspects within close orb are extremely important. Give conjunctions to angular house cusps and planets first choice, then squares that are exact or within one degree orb. Next in line is the opposition, followed by the rest of the aspects.

12

Aries Ascendant

| Cardinal | Fire |
| Positive | Ruler: Mars |

Aries is the natural ruler of the first house, the birthplace of new enterprises and beginnings. For this reason it is natural for an Aries rising individual to be more concerned with his own personal affairs than those of others.

Character Traits

The sign Aries on the cusp of the first house represents beginnings and youth. And, like the typical youth, Aries is impatient, impulsive and impetuous. Notice that all these adjectives begin with "I", the only person of concern to an Aries.

They are happiest when talking about themselves, and it is for this reason that they abhor idle gossip and are interested in only what concerns them and their immediate surroundings. Although they can be sympathetic at times, especially when they see someone being treated unjustly, they will go to any lengths and fight any battle to help another.

Aries individuals are strongly independent, optimistic and aggressive people who must be leaders in their sphere of life. They are ready to use force rather than tact to achieve their aims, giving others the impression that they are arrogant, forceful and difficult to deal with. In reality, Arians are immature youths, impatient to get their ideas across; this is the reason they cannot stand slow-witted people and do not like to deal with older persons who are more cautious and must think things out. An Aries never ponders his actions.

Aries individuals are so sure of themselves and their ideas that they take immediate steps to put them into action, and because of their ability to think fast their ideas are generally very good.

A lover of independence and often self-willed, an Aries needs to be a leader or in command of people or situations. Courageous and impulsive by nature, the Aries is not afraid of risky ventures. He will grasp new opportunities readily, even if he doesn't possess the knowledge required, because it is the challenging aspect of the situation that turns him on.

The nature is fiery and quick-tempered and Aries often overreacts to remarks made by others, no matter how slight or innocent they may be. Aggressiveness and undue striving for independence can impair one's success in life and possibly alienate those who would otherwise support him.

Arians must learn to control their restlessness, allowing proper time for plans to develop and never trying to force issues or rush into things before they are ready. They work well under pressure and their quick mental decisiveness makes them perfect for vocations where fast thinking is required, such as paramedic, police officer, firefighter, the military, emergency room nurse or doctor, or salesperson, or in the advertising field where new and different ideas are always required.

Physical Appearance

An individual will possess some of the Arian qualities and physical features if any of the following configurations are in the natal chart:
- Aries rising
- Mars in the first house (noticeably strong if conjunct the Ascendant)
- Mars within orb of the Ascendant's degree
- Ruler of the first house in Aries
- Ruler of the first house conjunct or otherwise in close aspect with Mars
- The Sun or Moon in Aries
- The Sun or Moon in close aspect with Mars
- Aries intercepted in the first house

Aries rising individuals will possess one or more of the following features:
- Mole, scar or blemish on head or face
- Ruddy or flushed complexion
- Reddish glint to the hair
- Long neck; sometimes men have an "Adam's Apple" in the throat area
- Deep creases at the sides of the mouth
- High forehead and bushy eyebrows that meet at the bridge of the

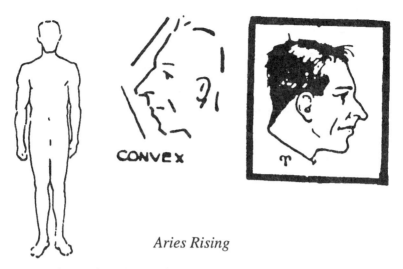

Aries Rising

nose (men often shave this area and women pluck their brows)
- Brisk walker and often leads with the head; fast talker
- Generates a lot of energy that may upset others who find it difficult to tolerate
- Convex or angular profile

Mentality

Clue words: Hasty, impatient, quick-tempered, brash, optimistic

The Aries mind is too hasty and impatient, wanting everything now, and will not wait for events to take place naturally. Instead, Aries individuals push their affairs with force and on impulse. If their ideas are blocked or hindered in any way, they will use force if necessary, and their words can be rather cutting and their tempers very short. Routine details are tolerated only if necessary as they prefer to start projects and get the ball rolling, leaving them to other people to finish. They initiate projects but lack the continuity to finish them.

Romantic Inclinations

Clue Words: Passionate, aggressive, jealous, possessive

Aries individuals are strongly sexual and passionate. Jealousy concerning a partner can cause them to lose their temper, possibly ending in separation. Aries women need men that are stronger in temperament or they soon lose respect for the partner. Although Aries women feel no man will ever dominate them, inwardly they yearn for one who has the ability to do so.

Health

They are prone to headaches, sinus conditions, colon and gall bladder problems, muscular aches and pains, cuts, burns and high fevers. They also can be accident prone, have a tendency to overwork and should wear protective eyewear if operating machinery. Inflammation may be experienced, especially in the face, and surgery is sometimes necessary, depending upon the aspect to Mars, ruler of the Aries Ascendant.

Parents of young children with Aries rising, Mars in the first house, Mars in aspect with the Ascendant degree or the child's ruling planet in Aries should guard against high fevers that could damage eyesight or hearing. They should act immediately to lower the temperature with a cool sponge bath.

Ascendant Ruler in Signs and Houses

Mars operates first through the sign position, which motivates its energy through the house in which it is posited. The aspects merely indicate how one will utilize the energy of Mars according to its sign position. The house position discloses either the people the natives must contend with or circumstances that will either be productive of success or create hindrances.

Mars, Ruler of the Ascendant, in the First House: Should Mars also be in Aries, the individual's success will depend solely upon his ability to control rash and impulsive behavior. With soft aspects to Mars in the first, these individuals are usually endowed with self-confidence, enterprise and industriousness. There is marked administrative ability and speedy execution of projects, which tends to ensure early success. As the planet Mars is accident prone, the native is likely to get a scar, mark or blemish on the head or face before reaching the teenage years.

Mars, Ruler of the Ascendant, in the First House in Taurus: The rash behavior is still present, but only after the native has exhausted his patience. In youth, these individuals should guard against throat infections that can develop into a serious situation and possibly affect the hearing. Sometimes the tonsils have to be removed during the early years.

Mars, Ruler of the Ascendant, in the Second House: Individual effort is likely to be the greatest factor in the acquisition of wealth, and money tends to be a big incentive toward the promotion of pet projects or personal endeavors.

Mars, Ruler of the Ascendant, in the Second House in Taurus: There is more patience with personal projects or situations in the acquisition of monetary gains. One may be more inclined to think twice before making an impulsive purchase or reaching an important decision involving finances or movable possessions.

Mars, Ruler of the Ascendant, in the Second House in Gemini: The mentality is quick to grasp new ideas and opportunities that will increase personal wealth. Sometimes there is more than one outlet for financial gain, holding down a full-time job with a possible sideline bringing in extra funds. Siblings may affect personal funds.

Mars, Ruler of the Ascendant, in the Third House in Gemini: There is mental alertness and executive ability backed by initiative and resourcefulness which facilitates early success. The argumentative disposition tends to produce frequent quarrels. There may be a strong urgency to write, teach, lecture or appear on radio or TV. One should be watchful of possible accidents to the hands, fingers and shoulders. Because they have nervous energy, some may smoke to relax. This my be risky as Gemini rules the lungs and damage could result later in life, possibly requiring surgery. Gemini can also operate on siblings who can either experience auto accidents or surgery of the lungs.

Mars, Ruler of the Ascendant, in the Third House in Cancer: These individuals are more sensitive and emotional than they would like others to believe. They often undergo emotional flareups, especially when they feel someone is being critical or making snide remarks about them. The areas to watch are the chest and stomach. It is possible a sibling may undergo surgery for cancer of the breast or stomach area.

Mars, Ruler of the Ascendant, in the Fourth House in Cancer: Regardless of gender, these individuals tend to wear the pants in the family. Much of this tendency for family control has been instilled by one of the parents and early environmental behavior patterns. Depending on the aspects, the male Arian could be good at home repair or remodeling as a profession. The female Arian may at some point give serious consideration to working with the general public in real estate, banking or the travel industry. Caution is advised when working with tools or around the home as accidents are possible and can occur there. Also, if Mars squares Pluto, a planet in the eighth house or the ruler of the eighth house, fires or other disasters are possible; keep home insurance up to date with adequate coverage. One of the parents may be a source of personal responsibility or domestic strife, or require surgery.

Mars, Ruler of the Ascendant, in the Fourth House in Leo: One of the parents may have a heart, eye or back problem at some point in life. Affairs of children may play an important role in connection with property. For example, the native may purchase a home for one of the children or co-sign for them. There is the likelihood of owning a bar, nightclub, sporting goods store or game room.

Mars, Ruler of the Ascendant, in the Fifth House in Leo: A good thing can be overdone and that is what these individuals often do. This can lead to stress resulting in heart problems, high blood pressure or chest pains, all symptoms of the necessity to slow down. Sports, gambling and entertainment are their forte. Male Arians make good physical education teachers, and this placement can produce a boy or an athletic girl. They can be impulsive and impetuous in love affairs, and should be careful in sports as accidents are possible. There is the capacity for loyal companionship, and leadership is likely to be the dominant principle.

Mars, Ruler of the Ascendant, in the Fifth House in Virgo: This tends to limit the amount of children as the native lacks patience with them. Sometimes one prefers dogs or cats to children and often treats them as such. Female Arians may get romantically involved with someone of a lower status or educational level. In either sex, they can be so selective in relationships that they often overlook the one real person who can make them happy.

Mars, Ruler of the Ascendant, in the Sixth House in Virgo: These individuals are inclined to do everything themselves, creating unnecessary fatigue and possible accidents. They would be wise to seek a vocation where there is freedom in movement and decision. Demanding perfection in others and being overly critical and fault-finding is par for the course. Arguments are possible with bosses or co-workers. Be careful with tools at work as accidents or injury can occur. Surgery may be necessary for ulcers or removal of moles.

Mars, Ruler of the Ascendant, in the Sixth House in Libra: Partnerships are likely to play an important role, and they may join forces in a teamwork environment to produce a certain type of service or commodity. Female Arians would be wise to avoid romantic relationships with coworkers, who are likely to be married. They have to drink a lot of water to maintain balance within the system and to avoid the formation of kidney stones.

Mars, Ruler of the Ascendant, in the Seventh House in Libra: The native seeks a partner who has the same type of energetic drive, ambition and self-confidence. These natives are not seeking a wallflower for a mate or partner, but desire someone who will work just as actively as they do toward a desired goal. However, when two individuals with the same temperament get together, it can lead to arguments. They need to learn they are dealing with independent people and should avoid the tendency to try to boss or dominate others. This placement generally endows an impetuous temperament that may precipitate strange domestic circumstances. Sometimes this indicates a hasty, early marriage.

Mars, Ruler of the Ascendant, in the Seventh House in Scorpio: With the ruling planet in the seventh house in Scorpio, these individuals are looking for someone with money or who has the capacity to attract it. The male Arian is also seeking a passionate, sexy female partner. However, little does he realize that this sexy partner can also be jealous, possessive and domineering. Because this is the ruling planet, Mars in Scorpio adds a strong secretive nature that can be vengeful when betrayed and often sarcastic and cutting in speech. This is a "do it my way or else" temperament.

Mars, Ruler of the Ascendant, in the Eighth House in Scorpio: This position generally endows forceful and stubborn character traits. These individuals are secretive, difficult to really know or understand. They may prefer to work with money obtained through the resources of others and are likely to inherit or gain financially through marriage. Many have to use force at some point in life to settle matters concerning insurance, social security, worker's compensation, income tax or alimony. They may have to learn early in life to properly channel sexual energy, and can have an explosive temper.

Mars, Ruler of the Ascendant, in the Eighth House in Sagittarius: The nature is less passionate due to possible moral and religious inclinations. Many become involved with legal matters concerning insurance settlements due to accidents. Money may be inherited through in-laws or obtained through working with distant matters, travel, educational pursuits or partnerships involving someone of a different nationality or background.

Mars, Ruler of the Ascendant, in the Ninth House in Sagittarius: Mental alertness is stimulated by a love of change and there is likely to be considerable fondness for a roving existence. Distant places, travel, legal issues, teaching, lecturing, higher education and being a perpetual student (one who is always taking classes for one thing or another) is certain to be a part of this native's existence from time to time. They may have to learn to control enthusiasm when sharing their knowledge with others as they can be quite aggressive in expressing their views, which can offend others. In-laws or those of foreign background may be a source of irritation and possible quarrels.

Mars, Ruler of the Ascendant, in the Ninth House in Capricorn: There is more emphasis on higher education. These individuals make good instructors because of their organizational ability and conscientious efforts to impart knowledge to those who want to learn. There may be more patience with teaching adults rather than elementary level children. Travel may be connected with work or visiting distant relatives. If the aspects are favorable to Mars, the native may do better in the business world away from the birthplace. High ranking officials or people of influence will touch upon these individuals and either promote or hinder career efforts.

Mars, Ruler of the Ascendant, in the Tenth House in Capricorn: These individuals fare better in their careers if they are permitted freedom of action and decision making. They do not function well under the control of someone who constantly watches or criticizes their every move. This is a blow hot, blow cold type of situation where Mars wants to forge ahead, but Capricorn always seems to place stumbling blocks in the path. Depending upon the aspects, this is a good placement for police officers, firefighters, military personnel or government workers. At times this placement can create dissension or arguments with bosses or parents.

Mars, Ruler of the Ascendant, in the Tenth House in Aquarius: The ruling planet in a fixed sign increases determination and willpower, which helps the individual accomplish whatever he sets out to do. Friends can be of unexpected help or assistance in the career. This placement usually gives excellent mechanical expertise, and these natives can come up with creative or inventive ideas along new and unique lines that draw favorable attention to their line of work. These individuals prefer a vocation where there is freedom of movement and independence in decision making because they have the power of a quick mentality. They may work with computers or electronics, or in the area of weather forecasting or the travel industry. Anything unique and different draws attention, especially if the hours are unstructured.

Mars, Ruler of the Ascendant, in the Eleventh House in Aquarius: These individuals may possess modern and progressive views, peculiar plans and unique ideas, and have a love of independence. They enjoy social contacts, and associations through friendships are important. They are likely to become personally involved with clubs and organizations and enjoy serving on the board of directors or holding an officer's position. They have to learn not to force their opinions on others unless invited to do so or strife could result. Male friends are likely to have mechanical ability or share a mutual interest in fields such as computers, electronics or astrology. There is a capacity for social leadership, and enthusiastic pursuit of pleasure usually helps to attract a wide circle of friends, particularly among people interested in sports and energetic activities.

Mars, Ruler of the Ascendant, in the Eleventh House in Pisces: Personal creative ideas, vivid impressions and uncanny intuition can guide these individuals into new inventive outlets that can lead to immeasurable benefits. Friends can vary from the creative artist, poet, musician or photographer to the type that drinks too much or is an abuser of drugs. Sometimes friends will use the native as a sounding board for their troubles. Others will pretend to be other than what they really are.

Mars, Ruler of the Ascendant, in the Twelfth House in Pisces: This is a touchy place and sign for Mars. If weak by aspect in the twelfth house, the individual could seek various means of escape which can be harmful, such as drug and alcohol abuse or clandestine affairs. Unless the aspects are favorable, women with this placement are likely to be hurt through deceptive love affairs or draw the wrong kind of male associations, such as the those who may take unfair advantage of them financially or emotionally. Men with this placement may feel a sense of inadequacy which can be connected to a lack of positive male parental guidance early in life. With either gender, with good aspects, this is an excellent placement for bartenders, barmaids, detectives, photographers, musicians, creative and imaginative writers or those in the medical field.

Mars, Ruler of the Ascendant, in the Twelfth House in Aries: No matter how you slice it, a female with this configuration will be hurt at sometime by a male companion. These individuals are overly sensitive, and will react too quickly to remarks made by others whether intentional or not. Men with Mars in the twelfth house are super-sensitive and may feel that something is wrong with them because they always seem to attract women who reject them. In either sign, Pisces or Aries, these individuals will come in contact with people who are mentally, emotionally or physically handicapped. They also may have something to do with large institutions, hospitals, jails, security police or investigative work. With good aspects there is considerable administrative ability that usually produces success.

Taurus Ascendant

Fixed   Earth
Negative   Ruler: Venus

Taurus is the Venus-ruled sign of the natural second house, with emphasis on creature comforts, finances and possessions. It is only natural that Taureans are concerned with security and personal welfare.

Character Traits

The main characteristic of the Taurus is the steadfast ability to stick with objectives until a goal has been reached. They have the willpower and perseverance to plod along despite great odds and obstacles.

Taureans realize the importance of first organizing and assimilating the proper material and knowledge before laying a firm foundation in any enterprise. Patient and sympathetic, they can never be pushed into a state of panic or be forced into making hasty decisions.

It is difficult for anyone to change the mind of a Taurus once it is made up. A Taurus may listen to another's suggestion, where the Aries will not, but this won't do anyone any good because Taurus will go ahead and do what he intended to do in the first place.

Never try to force or nag a Taurus into seeing the other side of an argument. They see only one side—their own—and if pushed too hard, have extremely explosive tempers. They seldom lose their tempers because they are basically people who dwell on peace and harmony. This is the reason they will not provoke arguments and, if they come across people they don't like or who annoy them, they avoid them.

Taureans have a strong love of beautiful things, luxury and comfort. They often display artistic and creative talents. Although they give others the impression of being materialistic or money-minded, this is because of their deep-rooted fear of insecurity. They use possessions and money as a sort of protective wall.

Because of their high integrity and reliability, many Taureans can be found in banking or in fields dealing with securities, mutual funds, real estate, commerce and finance. They also have a creative flair for work as beauty operators, interior decorators, the arts and so forth. Their sympathetic and stable nature fits them well for positions as doctors, nurses, teachers and social workers, and the earthy element often draws some into farming, ranching or the produce industry. Many are talented in art or music.

Self-reliant and generally easygoing, Taureans are persistent and stubborn by nature. They are attuned to practical and material matters, money and possessions. Basically kind and loving, they are inclined to be stubborn and jealous, resisting change.

Taureans have good staying power and persistence in the completion of methodical tasks. They are reserved and conservative, and faithfully follow their own line with perseverance and concentration.

Taureans may be slow learners, but they retain the knowledge once it is acquired. They can be agreeable, affectionate, sociable and loving, but also very unreasonable, prejudiced and bull-headed, stopping at nothing when angry. Good, hard workers, they are never overly expressive but maintain a silent ambition for personal success.

Physical Appearance

Individuals will possess some Taurus qualities and physical features if they have any of the following configurations in their natal chart:
- Taurus rising
- Venus in the first house (noticeably stronger if conjunct the Ascendant)
- Venus within orb of aspect with the Ascendant's degree
- Ruler of the first house in Taurus
- Ruler of the first house conjunct or otherwise in close aspect with Venus
- The Sun or Moon in Taurus
- The Sun or Moon in close aspect with Venus
- Taurus intercepted in the first house

Taurus rising individuals will possess one or more of the following features:
- Dimples in cheeks or cleft in chin
- Often, curly hair
- Full, short, thick neck
- Broad and heavy shoulders

  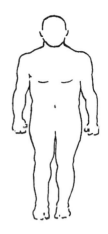

Taurus Rising

- Eyes prominent or slightly protruding with arched eyebrows
- Seldom bald
- Small ears; females may prefer to have ear lobes covered with hair
- Plumpness, especially later in life
- Square-built and average height
- Profile straight up and down

Mentality

Clue Words: Cautious, sluggish, deliberate, stable, dependable

The Taurus mind reacts slowly to outside influence and suggestions. For this reason some people regard them as somewhat dull or slow-witted when in reality they are slowly and deliberately digesting the information and making sure their move will be a wise one. Although the Taurus mind is one of the most practical, the psychological makeup is often connected with finances and material personal comforts.

Romantic Inclinations

Clue Words: Romantic, possessive, jealous, loyal and ardent

The Taurus individual is not aggressive in going after a romanic partner and prefers one who has money or knows the value of it. They like to entertain at home where they can show off their attractive surroundings. Once married, the mate of a Taurus must learn to accept a dull, routine life where words of endearment will not be frequently expressed. But in return the mate of a Taurus will have a steady, loyal person who will show love and affection through gentle tenderness and being an excellent provider.

Health

Taureans may have trouble with the throat, tonsils, vocal cords, larynx, thyroid gland, palate and the neck in general, and may experience goiter, croup, throat infections, laryngitis, mumps or cysts in the throat or jaw area. They may be more inclined to choke on food and should not talk while eating, as well as guarding against overindulgence in food and liquor. They should try to exercise more to improve circulation.

Ascendant Ruler in Signs and Houses

Venus, Ruler of the Ascendant, in the First House: Regardless of the sign, these individuals are socially conscious and like to have or attend parties. The women are, as a rule, attractive and retain their youthful appearance in later life, although they are apt to put on weight due to their love of candy, cake and cookies. Men with Venus in the first house are also attractive, and both sexes may have a cleft in the chin or dimples in the cheeks, adding to their handsome appearance. Depending on the aspect, there may be a dependency or a reliance upon others.

Venus, Ruler of the Ascendant, in Taurus in the First House: There is a strong stubborn streak in these natives. Money, possessions and gifts play an important part in their lives. They love flowers and may have a garden. Peace and harmony is important and disruptive influences in the immediate environment upset their emotional balance.

Venus, Ruler of the Ascendant, in the First House in Gemini: With favorable aspects, these individuals possess charm in public speaking and skill in writing or teaching. Manual dexterity can make them good hair stylists, telephone operators, secretaries, and radio and TV announcers. Small financial gains can be derived through business dealings or in cooperative efforts with women in general.

Venus, Ruler of the Ascendant, in the Second House in Gemini: More than one avenue of financial gain is possible. Men with this placement often receive gifts from young women. A sister or a brother with strong Venus coloring is apt to play an important role concerning personal finances. This is an excellent placement for owning a bookstore, operating a print shop, selling cosmetics or working for temporary placement agencies. There may be a tendency to purchase items in pairs—two pairs of shoes, two pairs of short, two belts, two telephones. Sometimes it is hard for them to resist a bargain, and they feel they have to pick up several of the item to make it worthwhile. They can be book collectors but prefer beautiful hardbound books to small softbound ones. Some may love to read romantic novels.

Venus, Ruler of the Ascendant, in the Second House in Cancer: Venus symbolizes gratuities and outright gifts, not prizes won in contests. Men with this placement often receive gifts or money through older women, or financial assistance through a parent, especially the mother. Women with this placement may work with older women who will assist them financially. Older women or those of Cancerian coloring can be quite generous with gifts, finery, jewelry and adornments. As a rule, this placement brings successful dealings with women in general, an increase in finances through the general public and a stimulation of creative activity.

Venus, Ruler of the Ascendant in the Third House in Cancer: These individuals make good diplomats, public relations personnel, hosts and receptionists. They are tactful, using finesse and diplomacy with phone calls, letters and general conversations. They are on friendly terms with siblings and, due to Cancer, may play a mothering role for them. Events and circumstances give these individuals much mental pleasure, and they have the ability to get along well with neighbors and close relatives. There is success in negotiations, contracts, agreements and through dealings with women.

Venus, Ruler of the Ascendant, in the Third House in Leo: Their speeches, gestures and letters have a certain dramatic flair, and they carry themselves well with an air of class about them. There is the ability to communicate with young people at their own level of understanding without giving the appearance of talking down to them. Depending on the aspects to Venus, the children of their siblings may play a major role in the lives of these natives. A sister or a brother with a strong Venus coloring (Taurus or Libra Moon, Sun or Ascendant, or Venus in the first house or in close aspect with the Ascendant, or the ruling planet in Taurus or Libra), may have a heart problem, high blood pressure or trouble with the eyes or back at some point in life.

Venus, Ruler of the Ascendant, in the Fourth House in Leo: Home is where the heart is, and that is true with Venus in the fourth house in Leo. These individuals love home surroundings that have a strong dramatic flair to them, such as those with a Spanish decor with an arched entrance and a metal, armored man on a pedestal near the fireplace. They love to entertain at home to show off their possessions, and are marvelous hosts and hostesses. They can become upset when the affairs of their children pose a threat to their tranquility and harmonious existence. There is the possibility that a female parent (or the father if he has a strong Venus or Leo coloring) will suffer heart, eye or back problems later in life.

Venus, Ruler of the Ascendant, in the Fourth House in Virgo: It is possible that an aunt will play a major role in the rearing of these natives, or perhaps they will spend the summer months at the home of an aunt or uncle. The aspects should indicate what role this aunt or uncle will play in the early environment. In some cases these natives may share their home or apartment with a coworker, but in any case they should always check the aspects before sharing their living quarters with anyone. Venus in the fourth house loves a harmonious and quiet environment; arguments and dissension will upset their sense of balance and throw them emotionally off course. Then the stressful situation starts to work on the stomach area, causing gastric upset and, in extreme cases, ulcers. These individuals love a neat home where there is place for everything an everything is in its place. They can get very upset when sharing their living quarters with someone who is sloppy and leaves clothes on the floor, the toothpaste uncapped, candy wrappers on the coffee table; this can turn them into nagging, critical shrews.

Venus, Ruler of the Ascendant, in the Fifth House in Virgo: Both sexes are discriminating and selective when it comes to romantic partners. They sometimes concentrate too much on physical appearance, dress and actions, overlooking what could have been a truly great marriage partner just because the person may be a casual dresser or possess some minor defect the native may find annoying. In the process of being too selective, they may run out of potential romantic partners and invariably end up with someone of a lesser status or background than their own. They have a creative flair that can be turned into a business if they put forth the effort. Women, for example, could be adept at cake decorating, dress designing, flower arranging or styling and trimming dogs. Men with this configuration could have a dramatic flair that is incorporated into their work. It is difficult for these natives to display affection to their children as they are always overly concerned with the child's health and welfare: Are they eating the right foods? Are they dressed warmly for the winter? There may be one child (a female child or a boy who has strong Venus or Virgo coloring) who will feign stomach ills whenever confronted with school problems or tests for which he or she has not studied.

Venus, Ruler of the Ascendant, in the Fifth House in Libra: These individuals have a dramatic flair for interior decorating, whether for the home or office. They are talented in the arts, music or dancing, but need a partner to help with decisions and promotion of their talents. Caution is necessary for there is the possibility of becoming romantically involved with married individuals.

Venus, Ruler of the Ascendant, in the Sixth House in Libra: A congenial work environment is important if these individuals are to function properly. They require attractive and harmonious surroundings. Women are likely to play an important role in their line of work. They may place emphasis on color coding file cards, folders and other work-related subject matter, and at some time a creative flair may be incorporated in the work. They strive for a harmonious relationship with coworkers, but should avoid the possibility of becoming romantically involved with married coworkers. Sometimes they may need to attend social affairs in connection with their employment. Whatever is produced is likely to fill a popular demand and draw special attention to their talents. Bonds of affection may be formed between the natives and those whose occupations are similar. In health it is important to drink a lot of fluid to maintain balance within the system and keep the kidneys properly flushed. Kidney stones, varicose veins and blood clots are possible health factors.

Venus, Ruler of the Ascendant, in the Sixth House in Scorpio: No matter what the profession, there is the urgency to be in control of people, machinery or situations. Care needs to be taken in dealing with coworkers and people with whom the natives come in contact through the place of employment, as they may be jealous of the natives' talents and work against them. Sexual problems may have a disturbing influence upon the natives' health and upset their ability to perform correctly at work. Women should avoid excessive hygiene of the female organs, as douching too much could result in irritation of the vagina. Some women may experience health problems with female organs, or be sensitive to birth control pills. Men may require surgery on the prostate or for hemorrhoids.

Venus, Ruler of the Ascendant, in the Seventh House in Scorpio: Situations involving marriage and business partnerships become important to the natives. This placement of Venus in Scorpio, however, colors the character traits to the extreme. Jealousy, possessiveness and dominance over the partner is often the rule. These natives also seek someone who is secretive, does not air the family linen and has money or good earning power. If Venus receives hard aspects, there is a possibility for men with this configuration to pay alimony or child support. Women with this placement who are betrayed will be determined to get even with the partner through his pocketbook and all mutual holdings. Both men and women can be extremely loyal, and expect the same in return.

Venus, Ruler of the Ascendant in the Seventh House in Sagittarius: With Taurus rising and the ruling planet in the mutable sign of Sagittarius, the natives are not as fixed in their ways as other Taurean individuals. The stubborn streak is there, but the natives know how to change their minds when they realize another approach is better. With the ruling planet in the seventh house in Sagittarius, they are more inclined to seek out partners with education beyond high school. If there are no adverse aspects to Venus, this is a good placement because partners will bring luck to the natives. Sometimes this placement leans toward marriage or a business partnership with someone from a different background, race or religion. Some tend to marry the same person twice, first in a civil ceremony and later in a religious one, or to renew their vows on the twenty-fifth wedding anniversary.

Venus, Ruler of the Ascendant, in the Eighth House in Sagittarius: As a rule, these individuals are honest in their financial dealings. Their manner is forthright, but they must be careful not to be too outspoken as they may unintentionally hurt the feelings of others with remarks that, although honest, should have been cushioned with softer words. Lady Luck shines on these natives as money often arrives at the last minute just when they are trying to figure out how to pay a past due bill. In-laws, people living in distant places or those who speak with a foreign accent can be generous with gifts or financial aid. Money may be gained through lawsuits involving an insurance company.

Venus, Ruler of the Ascendant, in the Eighth House in Capricorn: This is an earthy place for Venus, and individuals with this placement can be quite sexy and passionate. Women, however, feel they should receive something in return for their sexual favors, and it is for this reason that they may prefer older men, corporate types or others with power and money. Men with this configuration may prefer mature women or older ones, and are seeking a lady (Capricorn) by day who dresses distinctively and in good taste, but something of a prostitute (eighth house) by night. Sometimes men may experience trouble through a jealous, possessive woman. Because Venus rules Taurus and is placed in the partner's second house of money (eighth house), Taurus natives usually gain through the marriage partner.

Venus, Ruler of the Ascendant, in the Ninth House in Capricorn: This placement instills the importance of a college education. The natives are likely to carp on this theme because status, prestige and an influential career position cannot be achieved on a high school education. These are lovely people in spite of the Capricorn signature, reserved and aloof, yet honorable in their dealings with others. In-laws may pose a problem during the early stages of marriage, but as time progresses, a kinship slowly develops that leads to an expression of deep fondness. These individuals may move away from their place of birth or seek careers in different states. Travel is usually connected with practical purposes or through vocational duties.

Venus, Ruler of the Ascendant, in the Ninth House in Aquarius: Writers of lovely, well-versed books on unique subjects, they may take up the study of astrology, weather forecasting or computer programming, or work in the travel industry or host seminars or psychic fairs. Travel is generally tied with groups of people—group tours, lecturing at conferences or attending seminars. Outgoing with a witty and unusual sense of humor, they are certain to come in contact with people from all walks of life. If Venus is afflicted natally, separation through divorce is possible or legal matters may be connected with a female. They may take up the study of art, music or singing. Likely to mix socially with one or more people from abroad or with well-educated individuals, financial gains can be had through publications, travel or lawsuits.

Venus, Ruler of the Ascendant, in the Tenth House in Aquarius: These individuals need a profession where they can call their own shots. Although a 9-to-5 job is boring to them, they can tolerate it for the money. The greatest pleasure is in being in the public eye, especially in occupations in the entertainment field. Social contacts may be connected with the job, such as in public relations or in serving as a host for a conference. Astrology and the unique professions draw their interest. When the aspects are favorable from major transits to Venus in the tenth house, women can be of assistance in the career, and in some cases these natives may enter into a business arrangement with a female friend. Men who have Venus in Aquarius may want to keep women in the platonic state and avoid marriage because they prefer to concentrate on promoting their career goals. The arts, movies, acting, singing and appearances on radio or TV are just a few of the outlets that may interest the Taurus rising person.

Venus, Ruler of the Ascendant in the Tenth House in Pisces: The creative arts may still be present, but much depends on the conditioning of the natal twelfth house, planets therein, the ruler thereof and aspects thereto. Otherwise the interest may be in the medical field or with pharmaceutical products. Some may be drawn to owning or working in bars. Hospitals, institutions, jails and detective work are another interesting factor that may enter into Taurus career choices. One always has to be careful of reputation, keeping standards above board and avoiding attempts to get to the top of the profession with quickie schemes. Women can be silent contributors to the profession or turn into secret enemies who try to discredit the reputation. In some cases, Taurus individuals may come in contact with or work with people who are mentally, emotionally or physically handicapped.

Venus, Ruler of the Ascendant, in the Eleventh House in Pisces: These individuals have unique, creative and inventive talent in the fields of art, music, writing or dancing. They should be careful of becoming entangled with those with peculiar emotional or sexual ideas as they may have a harmful effect on the position and reputation of these natives, who cry at the drop of a hat and are easy prey for a sob story. Others sense this vulnerability and are likely to take unfair advantage of these natives or use them as a sounding board for their troubles. People see these individuals as trusting souls, but do not know that once betrayed they will never again associate with them socially. Whatever arouses the feelings of these natives depends on the state of their emotional sensitivity at the time, and the favorable indications of Venus simply mean they will be more often prompted to active responses by a sensitivity to harmonious, beautiful and endearing things than by more unpleasant or distasteful ones. At times, friends and even casual acquaintances may go out of their way with gifts to show how much they think of these natives. Many of the natives' hopes and wishes can become radiant realities through the art of visualization, viewing in their mind's eye what they hope to achieve and then letting the subconscious mind lead them toward that goal.

Venus, Ruler of the Ascendant, in the Twelfth House in Aries: These natives may wish to hold officer positions in clubs or organizations as they prefer to play the leading role rather than that of a follower. They have an inner intuitive knowledge of which individuals can be of help to them, and they set out to be their friends. There may be one particular friend with an Arian quality, perhaps with a mole, scar or mark on the head or face, who will enter the lives of these natives and play an important role. They love to circulate and enjoy a large company of friends. Men with this configuration will be attracted to women who are different, independent and decisive. The achievement of their hopes and wishes depends on the personal energy they put forth to accomplish their desired goals.

Venus, Ruler of the Ascendant, in the Twelfth House in Aries: These natives can be quite vulnerable when it comes to sexual and emotional involvements with the opposite sex. Their super-sensitivity to discordant environments can push them into losing their tempers because they can't stand undue noise, confusion and disruptive influences, all of which tends to unsettle their sense of balance and make them highly nervous. Working at a job where they are left alone is preferred as they do their best work in quiet solitude with no interruptions. Hospitals, jails and the military will touch their lives, and someone who is emotionally, mentally or physically unbalanced will enter their lives and create emotional disturbances. A lack of self-confidence may be the prevailing problem that causes these natives to overreact to statements they misinterpret, and thus lash out in temper, much to everyone's surprise.

Venus, Ruler of the Ascendant in the Twelfth House in Taurus: There is the possibility with this placement of having a learning, hearing or speech impediment. Some kind of drawback keeps these natives from full self-expression, or they may enjoy being alone, preferring to entertain only a few select friends in the home. Depending on the aspects, those that feel exploited by another, a boss or a company which employs them, perhaps feeling underpaid for their work, may borrow things to compensate for this lack—for example, taking home paper, pencils or other minor office supplies. In extreme cases, those who work for physicians, for example, may even try to alter the books so they will be able to hold back some of the cash from patients to make up for what they feel is inadequate pay. In other instances they may experience hidden elements and deception involving money matters in which they are cheated out of money or possessions that are rightfully theirs.

Gemini Ascendant

| Mutable | Air |
| Positive | Ruler: Mercury |

Gemini is the Mercury-ruled sign of the natural third house, which has to do with communications and short travels. It is instinctive for these individuals to go places and express themselves, vocally or through the written word.

Character Traits

The main characteristic of Gemini is adaptability in almost any given situation. They possess both manual and mental dexterity, giving them the ability to handle a great variety of tasks, and often simultaneously.

The nature is restless and full of nervous energy, and the attention span is short because they bore easily. These natives must be constantly on the move, doing things, visiting friends and talking, which they do in an easy flowing manner. Able to manipulate their words to a high degree of persuasion, they often succeed in discovering valuable bits of information or secrets from others. Gemini people are not deceitful, but rather are improvisers who either change or leave out sources of information to best suit their purposes.

The dualistic nature of Gemini makes it extremely difficult for others to understand them. At times they are charming, interesting and full of good humor, and at other times the attitude will be completely different—moody, irritable, full of sarcasm or cynical—leaving others to wonder what they said or did to make them act that way.

Active, both mentally and physically, there is a strong desire for variety and change, and they are capable of engaging in more than one project at a time. This dual trait can scatter the forces, thereby producing little progress and ending in wasted effort.

Geminis must keep busy as inactivity creates impatience and boredom, and there is a need to talk and meet people. However, they seldom get beneath the surface or really get to know the inner nature of their acquaintances.

They often worry about insignificant things rather than major issues, and some are unable to turn off their minds at night, constantly rehashing the events of the previous day, thus interfering with the needed rest their systems require.

Geminis collect facts and data and continually change from one set of facts to the next, often without digesting them or arriving at any real conclusion. Quick at learning and good transmitters of knowledge, they make good teachers, lecturers and writers of short articles. They are unable to come up with their own ideas and need someone to assist with subjects to write about.

Due to their natural talkative ability and quick wittedness, they are well suited for such occupations as teacher, lecturer, salesperson, journalist, radio or TV announcer, comedian or writer of short stories or plays. They require jobs where they have complete freedom of movement without dull routine, where each day holds exciting challenges for them.

Physical Appearance

Individuals will possess some of the Gemini qualities and physical features if they have any of the following configurations in the natal chart:
- Gemini rising
- Mercury in the first house (noticeably stronger if conjunct the Ascendant)
- Mercury within orb of aspect with the ascending degree
- Ruler of the first house in Gemini
- Ruler of the first house conjunct or otherwise in close aspect with Mercury
- Sun or Moon in Gemini
- Sun or Moon in close aspect with Mercury
- Gemini intercepted in the first house

Gemini rising individuals possess one of more of the following features:
- High forehead, often accompanied by a sharp angle or bump just below the hairline
- Long, straight nose that protrudes from the face
- Gemini females may wear their hair parted in the middle; others wear it pulled back in a ponytail or bun

Gemini Rising

- Quick, alert and expressive eyes
- Nervous hand gestures with hands constantly moving; often clicks the top of the pen off and on, or folds bits of paper into tiny pieces
- Some smoke to calm the nervous system
- Usually a tall, slender body
- May have long arms, legs and fingers
- Walks with quick, alert steps

Mentality

Clue Words: Witty, intelligent, spontaneous, intuitive, cunning

The Gemini mind is quick and versatile, but without perseverance as it tends to flit from one subject to another. This gives the impression that these natives are highly informed when actually they are only skimming the surface; they don't have the staying power to go deeply into any one subject.

"Jack of all trades, master of none" may be their slogan unless they develop strength of character and learn to finish one project before going on to another. Their minds must be kept busy and constantly stimulated with various hobbies and projects; otherwise, the lower nature takes over and the cynical, sly Gemini trends develop.

Romantic Inclinations

Clue Words: Fickle, changeable, two-faced, charming, exciting

Geminis have a highly sexual nature, but it is short lived because they don't have the patience or want to take the time to be great lovers. Seldom is one romantic partner able to fulfill all the variety of interests that keep a highly nervous Gemini on the go. It is for this reason that they often seek more than one companion at a time.

Health

They tend to become depressed easily and at times may exaggerate or become overly concerned about health matters. Geminis can become hypochondriacs. Areas for concern are the arms, hands, shoulders and lungs.

Ruler of the Ascendant in Signs and Houses

Mercury, Ruler of the Ascendant in the First House in Gemini: Quickness of wit and mental ingenuity tend to be strongly marked. There is likely to be a vital love of knowledge, devotion to study and interest in literary pursuits. Adaptability is a striking feature. They may love to read and be collectors of books. Because Mercury is a barren planet in a barren sign, the native may be an only child; but much depends upon the condition of the third house, planets therein, its ruler and aspects. They usually are dexterous and are good at working with the printed or spoken word—journalism, teaching, writing, lecturing, salesmanship. Interested in new ideas and the changes these ideas bring about, these individuals are quick in speech, thought and action. They may have the tendency at times to misinterpret others. In the negative sense they can be highly nervous, restless, lacking in sympathy, nitpicky and impractical.

Mercury, Ruler of the Ascendant, in the First house in Cancer: Ultra-sensitive to critical and faultfinding remarks made by others, even though they are offered in the constructive sense, some may turn to food to calm their emotional hurts, and while eating may rehash what was said and done and how the native should have retaliated. If Mercury in Cancer receives hard aspects, especially from Saturn or the rulers of the fourth or tenth houses, the native may psychologically feel that a parent favored a brother or sister. The parent may deny this, yet the native feels inwardly that this is so. Due to the need to escape from hurt feelings through food, there may be a weight problem.

Mercury, Ruler of the Ascendant, in the Second House in Cancer: There is an intuitive knowledge and feeling for what the general public needs. For example, an individual who works in a restaurant will sense when a customer is desirous of another cup of coffee or, if at a buyer's market, the individual can portend what clothing may interest the general public in the next season. This is an excellent placement for mass communication by speech or writing, and advertising, journalism and creative writing can be a good source of income. Some may enter the sales field in real estate, the food industry, catering or operating a carryout beverage store. Sometimes gain comes from a profession or an occupation in which the person acts as go-between; this often is highly lucrative. They can be good money managers and should consider financial careers. Financial gain may come through a parent, and they have a strong desire to own a home for security reasons. They may have a small amount of money hidden in various places, such as dollar bills clipped to the car's sun visor or in a compartment, a piggy bank or other container. It doesn't have to be a large sum—just enough to give a sense of security that there is something on hand for an emergency. When these natives run into a mental block and must produce something written on the job, eating something with a little sugar can help stimulate the mind, even if it's just a piece of candy.

Mercury, Ruler of the Ascendant, in the Second House in Leo: They prefer quality goods, and may spend impulsively on luxury items. These natives make good teachers for they have the ability to communicate well with young people at their own level. There may be a desire to hold a management or supervisory position, Gambling, sports, entertainment, nightclubs, the theater, affairs of children (not necessarily their own) or a romantic interest may have some effect on personal finances.

Mercury, Ruler of the Ascendant, in the Third House in Leo: With Gemini on the Ascendant, the third house is always a source for serious consideration and, no matter what sign the native has on the Ascendant, check the house that Mercury governs in the natal chart. Mercury in the third house in Leo is an excellent placement for this planet. When Gemini mutability is coupled with Leo fixity, the individuals become engulfed in more than one project, but the one that holds the most interest (Leo) will be given more time and energy. This placement enhances the need to communicate, which will be done with dramatic flair and extensive hand gestures. The ego (Leo) needs to be expressed through the spoken and written word. They make excellent speakers, being flamboyant and illustrative, and may work in the theater. Wherever they can create a stage, they will perform. An optimistic outlook tends to enhance the mental faculties and encourages a love of study. There is likely to be considerable practical ability and success. A sibling may have a heart, back or eye problem, and the native should also guard against any possible injury to those areas of the body, taking care of the health before a flareup becomes a chronic condition.

Mercury, Ruler of the Ascendant, in the Third House in Virgo: Unless very well aspected, this is not the best sign for Mercury. A mutable planet in a mutable house in a mutable sign makes for high nervous tension. These natives are quick to criticize or find fault with others, and can be nagging nitpickers. They may only touch the surface of a subject as they lack the patience to get to the core of things. At some point in life they may have to file papers for health benefits, worker's compensation or sick leave. There may be problems with coworkers or bosses whom they feel are too detail-minded or whose system of doing things is not correct in comparison with the way these natives feel things should be done. Because Mercury is a barren planet and is in a semi-barren sign, these natives may be only children.

Mercury, Ruler of the Ascendant, in the Fourth House in Virgo: Nothing makes these Gemini Ascendant people happier than to operate a small business or sideline from their home. Check the sixth house (Mercury in Virgo) to see if the Moon (natural ruler of the fourth house) is positioned there or if Mercury makes an aspect to a planet in the sixth house or to the ruler of the sixth house; if so, at some point the native will work at home. There is a strong possibility that these natives may live temporarily with an aunt or uncle or share their living quarters with someone encountered through their place of employment. Home conditions are likely to assume undue importance and the environment may cause much mental anxiety. They may not approve of something their mother or father did during their formative years, which in turn could have had an effect on the nervous system. These natives must be as conscientious a possible in their dealings with the outside world. Self-control and attention to detail are the character traits that will allow them to accomplish their aims.

Mercury, Ruler of the Ascendant, in the Fourth House in Libra: Lack of harmony and frequent arguments between parents during formative years or an unusual living arrangement within the home could upset the balance within the system and create a bed-wetter (Libra rules the kidneys). This can be confirmed if Mercury is in hard aspect with the Moon, natural ruler of the fourth house. These individuals make good judges, counselors, astrologers or attorneys because they can be impartial when making decisions; however, they may have trouble making decisions concerning their own affairs. Never ask children with this combination if they want vanilla or chocolate ice cream as they will probably take a scoop of each rather than make a decision. There is a tendency to balance situations or circumstances. If these natives owe someone ninety-eight cents, they will give the individual one dollar and tell him to keep the change because the dollar represents an even, round figure. They don't like contending with odds and ends, and color will have an important effect upon their home decor.

Mercury, Ruler of the Ascendant, in the Fifth House in Libra: Refinement tends to be an important characteristic. There may be ability for drama or acting, and children (not necessarily the native's own) and romance usually play a large part in the life and have special meaning. The marriage partner may have children by a previous marriage, and these natives may become romantically involved with married people. There is creative talent for writing romance novels and a dramatic flair in the field of art, music or dancing. These individuals are good hostesses and planners of social affairs. They could be sympathetic and unbiased listeners or school counselors.

Mercury, Ruler of the Ascendant, in the Fifth House in Scorpio: If Leo is on Gemini's natural third house with the ruler Mercury in Scorpio in the fifth house, children or a romantic interest could be a source of great mental anxiety. These natives should avoid co-signing a mortgage agreement for a child or obtaining a loan for a romantic partner; in all probability, the natives will suffer a financial loss. Men and women may have to deal with a lot of paperwork connected with a child's medical records, hospitalization insurance forms or child support. Romantic partners may be too preoccupied with the sexual aspect of romance rather than the affectionate side. The nature is jealous and possessive and, once hurt or betrayed by a lover, their thoughts center on ways to seek revenge. The Gemini rising individual can be quite talkative, but the ruling planet in Scorpio will seldom reveal anything of a personal nature.

Mercury, Ruler of the Ascendant, in the Sixth House in Scorpio: Individuals with this configuration can be adept at manipulating others to work voluntarily for their cause or organization. Without a doubt there is skillful ability to sway the masses, and public speaking is a talent. Research, the occult or the medical field are good choices for employment, and these individuals may have to deal with paperwork connected with payroll or scheduling of employee hours or duties. Other people's funds may in some way have a bearing on employment issues. Health matters demand selectivity in the choice of sexual partners who may pass on dangerous viruses. The reproductive organs and those that deal with the elimination process need to be cleansed properly to avoid possible bladder infections. Women may experience sensitivity to birth control pills, and men may require surgery on the prostate or for hemorrhoids.

Mercury, Ruler of the Ascendant, in the Sixth House in Sagittarius: With a mutable sign rising and Mercury in a mutable sign, there is a strong degree of internal restlessness and desire for change. These natives will have to be careful not to overtax the mental capacity or to let the mind wander along superficial aims or impossible attainments. They are always busy, busy, busy with a lot of paperwork and details, often related to their jobs, health benefits or worker's compensation. These individuals should avoid taking on too many projects and scattering their forces; instead, they should determine their priorities and try to complete the most important ones first. If they are not teachers, they will at some time play the role of instructor, perhaps teaching others certain aspects of their jobs. Printing presses, copy machines, books, printed material or lecturing, and the necessity for travel due to employment, will all play a role in their personal activities. They may come in contact with people from all walks of life or those living in distant cities as a result of their careers.

Mercury, Ruler of the Ascendant, in the Seventh House in Sagittarius: Popularity in literary and scientific circles can lead to success. Partnerships are likely to be important factors in connection with the occupation, especially an alliance with a younger person. With the ruling planet in the seventh house, they seek marriage partners who have similar interests in sports, outdoor recreation, travel and intellectual pursuits. If potential marriage or business partners lack intelligence or cannot hold decent conversations, the natives may soon drop them. When travel is necessary, it is unlikely that Geminis go unaccompanied. Mental awareness is stimulated by partnership matters and they are generally at their best when dealing with partners in business affairs. Due to a short attention span, there may be reliance on others to help with written material.

Mercury, Ruler of the Ascendant, in the Seventh House in Capricorn: Mingling with the upper crust and associating with people of influence characterizes this placement, which can produce a May-December relationship. In the early years they may be drawn to older, mature or professional partnerships in marriage or business. As they begin to mature, however, they lean toward the younger generation, as if they hope to recapture their youth or feel they have had enough of the serious-minded type of individual and desire to be free from restrictive relationships. Mercury in Capricorn can add a hard core to the nature, making the native aloof, reserved, cold, detached and standoffish. There may be health problems with the teeth, skin or bony structure of the body.

Mercury, Ruler of the Ascendant, in the Eighth House in Capricorn: Sedentary occupations in partnership, or some form of literary or scientific work, are the most promising sources of gain. Financial benefits may also come through marriage or a legacy. Men with this placement may have a mental, detached attitude about sex, viewing it only as a necessity to relieve sexual tension. Once sex is over, they are already thinking about a business deal or important contacts that have to be made. Some women with this placement may also have a detached view of sex, seeing nothing wrong in the exchange of sexual favors for monetary gifts. Mutual funds will play a definite role in the lives of these natives, and it may not be uncommon for them to place influence and earning power above romance in their choice of a marriage partner. At some point in life, a very powerful, influential and possibly political figure will have an effect on joint financial gains.

Mercury, Ruler of the Ascendant, in the Eighth House in Aquarius: This placement has a more positive influence than Capricorn. The Gemini person can gain financially through the most unique circumstances and sometimes just being in the right place at the right time. Friends, clubs and organizational activities may influence financial gain or loss depending on the aspects in force at the time. Dealing with organized labor unions, associations, computers, video equipment or CDs, or putting on conventions or psychic fairs can produce monetary gain. Should Aquarius be on the ninth house cusp rather than intercepted in the eighth house, money may arrive unexpectedly from distant places. In any case, there is the likelihood of fluctuation of finances, bringing in periods of plenty followed by times of lean. Friends can be a source of financial backing in connection with a pet project or an invention.

Mercury, Ruler of the Ascendant, in the Ninth House in Aquarius: There is a strong interest in unique and different subjects, including astrology, electronics, weather forecasting and the travel industry. Attending seminars, conferences or lectures in various distant places can enhance mental attributes and expertise. If traveling by air, these natives should always check the transits affecting Mercury in Aquarius in the ninth house for possible delays or trouble with flights. Mercury in Aquarius will bring these individuals in touch with small commuter planes. Depending on the aspects to Mercury in Aquarius, something may be physically wrong with a brother- or sister-in-law who may have a health problem that is difficult to cure, such as multiple sclerosis, lupus, paralysis or another illness that impairs the nerves and muscle structures of the body.

Mercury, Ruler of the Ascendant, in the Ninth House in Pisces: The psychic and intuitive ability can be quite accurate at times and at other times unreliable. In spite of this, these natives should listen to inner warnings of caution, and verify travel plans when flying in case of delays or cancellations due to fog or severe weather conditions. With Mercury in Pisces, a mutable sign, they should avoid the tendency to worry and scatter the forces by engaging in numerous activities instead of concentrating on one thing until completed. There may be too much doubt and not enough decision making. There may be confusion or complex matters in connection with clerical or legal affairs, and troublesome journeys can be avoided by paying close attention to maps and detours. Travel is likely to be an important factor and the occupation may be linked with it in some way. An in-law may have a mental, emotional or physical problem. These natives may drink too much or require medication to correct a health problem, and they should be careful of food and water intake while in foreign countries, or in an environment that is different from the norm, to avoid physical and dietary upsets.

Mercury, Ruler of the Ascendant, in the Tenth House in Pisces: Photos of these natives will appear before the public, even if just in the office newsletter. Resourceful and great mental activity are conducive to the necessary ability for coping with the contingencies of life. Business ability is usually strong and success can come through vivid self-expression. The goal in life for these natives is to be recognized by others and hold a high ranking career position of esteem and status. Ideas, plans and mental powers are directed outside the home and into business, politics and public life. Vocational tendencies and abilities may be determined by delineating the planet in most powerful and closest aspect to Mercury and treating that planet as though it were actually in the tenth house. The mind is intuitive with an uncanny knack for sensing when to make the right moves at the most opportune time, especially in connection with business or career. From time to time these natives may discover that those they have befriended through their line of work are not what they appeared to be, and may even develop secret enemies. They may alter or change a few letters in their names, or use a *nom de plume* to enhance their image.

Mercury, Ruler of the Ascendant, in the Tenth House in Aries: These individuals are quick to grasp and undertake new opportunities even if they have little knowledge of the project in mind; the challenge is what holds the Gemini's interest. With active, penetrating, adaptable minds that are used resourcefully in business, these people have a bent for literary work or agenting, but want to hold executive or administrative positions. They may teach, write or lecture, or work for a newspaper or in the printing or trucking industry. All forms of clerical and secretarial work come under this configuration. Studies pertinent to the profession may have to be undertaken. Mental hardness develops, whereby others are not permitted beyond a certain point in trust. This can concern a repetition of unfair tactics or dishonesty through those in the workplace, especially if they have instilled a deep sense of personal hurt.

Mercury, Ruler of the Ascendant, in the Eleventh House in Aries: Intellectual keenness tends to enhance the reputation in connection with societies and associations. They prefer to hold leading positions in the operational affairs of any club or organization, and are likely to devote their mental powers to getting people together for a common objective to exchange views or ideas. Companions are sought more on the mental rather than the emotional plane. They shouldn't rely on too much help or assistance through friends, as Aries is the sign that forces one to handle matters personally. These individuals may become involved with the type of friends who are interested in improving their intellectual abilities. Because this is the third house of the ninth house, news of jury duty is likely at some time.

Mercury, Ruler of the Ascendant, in the Eleventh House in Taurus: At some point these individuals may come in contact with wealthy or financially well-off friends who may offer assistance in promoting an invention or a personal endeavor. Some Gemini individuals may hold positions within a club or organization in which they handle monetary affairs; if so, they should be careful in handling the funds and keep up-to-date records as one so-called friend may accuse them of mismanagement of the club's money. With Mercury in a fixed sign, there is less of a tendency to scatter the forces; although dual activities will still take place, those that hold promise of financial gain will be completed.

Mercury, Ruler of the Ascendant, in the Twelfth House in Taurus: These natives should listen to their intuition as it could provide a good source of protection regarding financial matters. In some instances relatives or siblings can become enemies and enmity can be experienced from close neighbors for a variety of reasons, including calls to the police. Check the third house (natural house of Mercury) and the second house (Mercury in Taurus) to determine if there is the possibility that a brother or sister may be deceptive regarding personal possessions or money that rightfully belongs to the native. They should avoid get-rich-quick schemes for there is a tendency to try to make money the easy way. If necessary, the natives should isolate themselves to avoid interruptions when trying to create something of esoteric value. Although they abhor confusion and chaotic conditions, it is nevertheless part of their existence and from time to time they must learn to cope with disruptive influences, noise or arguments. Care should be taken not to mismanage the funds of others, especially a physician or if handling funds connected with hospitals or charitable institutions.

Mercury, Ruler of the Ascendant, in the Twelfth House in Gemini: These natives may employ their minds in a highly intuitive way and have great interest in exploring psychic, occult or past life matters. They should be careful of creating enmity through personal criticism of others through speech or writing. There is a love of mystery and secret affairs or adventures, and they need to take time out to rest the nervous system through quietude and seclusion. Emotional stress can disturb the mental balance, bring mental uneasiness and, in the extreme, a condition of hypochondria. On occasion, there will be a need for discretion in the expression of personal opinions and views, both in speech and correspondence, as an unwise word can result in trouble, especially if letters fall into the wrong hands. In some cases, secret communications, trips and consultations are possible, and unsigned letters or phone calls of a harmful nature may be received.

Cancer Ascendant

Cardinal   Water
Passive   Ruler: Moon

Cancer is the Moon-ruled sign of the natural fourth house, which is the nurturing place for inner security, home, family and emotional sensitivity.

Character Traits

Cancer is on the cusp of the fourth house in the natural zodiac and represents emotional stability or instability that is a product of early environment and parental influence.

There may be a close attachment to one of the parents or a strong dislike of them. Often referred to as the orphan of the signs, these individuals may lose one of their parents early in life through death, separation or abandonment. In some instances it is a matter of non-communication between parent and child or lack of emotional response and affection to the point where the child feels cut off or detached from the parent.

The main characteristic of Cancerians is their receptiveness to the moods and feelings of others, for they possess a nature that is both sympathetic and sensitive. Their one drawback is their deep-rooted fear of insecurity, not only financial, but also emotional. It is for this reason they tend to withdraw into their crab-like shell at the slightest hint of rejection or criticism from others, no matter how constructive it was meant to be. There is a tendency to brood or dwell on these past slights or hurts and the Cancerian is likely to rehash, over and over, what they "should" have said in response. While they are in this state of mind, they may turn to eating, perhaps a glass of milk and a piece of apple pie as balm to their emotional hurts. For some, there is a need to own a home for the sake of inner security.

Cancerians like to collect things and desire material objects, holding on to them for sentimental reasons. They like new clothes, but have difficulty giving away those that are old or outdated. Some are good cooks, but most Cancerians cook only for survival reasons and would rather eat out.

Cancerians will work hard if they have to, but wish for someone to enter their lives and support them so they can pursue a position that allows them to work at home.

The inborn fear of financial insecurity has many of them hiding money in odd places—car, sugar bowl, piggy bank, bottom of a purse. It does not have to be a large sum—just some small change to let them know they have something to fall back on in a crisis. It should be no surprise that many of the country's great money-makers are Cancerians.

Cancerians can be overly protective and possessive of their immediate family, children and home possessions, and should guard against being too self-sacrificing, very often considering themselves martyrs. They often have excellent recall of childhood memories with fertile imaginations that are an inspiration for writing.

Their interest in history, family heritage and traditions suits them favorably for such occupations as antique dealer, coin and stamp collector and in such fields where they can serve the general public—medicine, nursing, social and welfare work or public speaking. The food industry is another outlet, and anything to do with real estate, homes and furnishings brings out their natural affinity for the domestic lines.

Physical Appearance

Individual possess some of the Cancer qualities and physical features if any of the following configurations in the natal chart:
- Cancer rising
- Moon in the first house (stronger if conjunct the Ascendant)
- Moon within orb of aspect with the Ascendant's degree
- Ruler of the first house in Cancer
- Ruler of the first house conjunct or otherwise in close aspect with the Moon
- Sun or Moon in Cancer
- Sun in close aspect with the Moon
- Cancer intercepted in the first house

Cancer rising individuals possess one or more of the following features:
- Top heavy; upper part of the body may be larger than the lower
- Medium height with a strong, well-set body

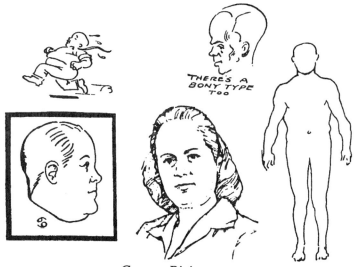

Cancer Rising

- Men usually have a soft, feminine appearance
- Round, moon-shaped face with pale complexion and small features
- May walk with a rolling gait or sometimes sideways and then sort of turns left or right to the desired destination
- Obesity can contribute to weight gain
- Short, turned-up nose
- Arms hanging from the side sometimes curve in to a crab-like position
- Feet and hands are small and delicate
- Children who suck their thumbs often come under Cancer rising

Mentality

Clue Words: Imaginative, hypersensitive, nurturing, insecure

The Cancerian mind has excellent memory recall and draws upon past experiences to use as a guide when similar conditions arise. They have fertile imaginations and a sentimental and sympathetic nature. Extremely sensitive to criticism, they will rehash in their minds, over and over, the hurt that was perpetrated upon them. Their minds operate more through feelings and emotions than logic. There is love for the past, family traditions, the fireside, apple pie and whatever else makes up a comfortable home atmosphere.

Romantic Inclinations

Clue Words: Possessive, clinging, emotional, protective, considerate

Due to fear of rejection, the romantic Cancerian seldom expresses personal feelings to another individual until certain that it is being reciprocated. When a date has to be canceled, often for good reasons, the Cancerian immediately takes the negative view and regards it as a form of rejection. The imagination is so strong that they tend to be overly romantic and sentimental, one reason why they get hurt so easily, especially when the other individual wants a platonic relationship.

Health

Cancer rules the stomach, breasts and digestive organs. The one main fault is the tendency to exaggerate illness. Their imaginative minds dwell on pain and expands it out of proportion, sometimes creating the very thing they fear, so they must always keep an optimistic view and immediately see a physician when health problems persist. Emotions should be kept under control. To ease their frustrations when minor unpleasant incidents occur, they may unconsciously eat even when they are not hungry. But when major events occur, they are more likely to avoid eating because food can upset them. In either case these practices can be a detriment to their health and well being.

Ascendant Ruler in Signs and Houses

Moon, Ruler of the Ascendant, in the First House: If the Moon is in the first house in any sign, emotions, feelings and sensitivity to all nearby persons and conditions play a major role. These individuals seek professions in which there is direct contact with the public, such as banking, real estate, food industry, astrology or nursing. Food or food products almost always come in contact with these natives. These women make excellent hostesses and cooks. No matter the occasion, they insist on bringing something to the festivities. I have a male client with the Moon in Virgo in the first house who was a cook on board ship in the navy. Although he hates to cook, he does so out of necessity since his wife died and left him with two school age children. The Moon governs an older woman who will in some way influence the early environment during the formative years. This could be a mother, grandmother, aunt or teacher. Men with this placement seem to gravitate toward older women for companionship, or women of their own age who are mothers of young children. Some of these women are apt to be married and if the Moon receives hard aspects, the man could become emotionally involved and hurt in this unwise affair. Either sex will certainly do their share of traveling. There is also a likelihood of a close attachment to one of the parents, usually the mother. But I discovered that one woman had close ties with a Cancer rising father so the Moon in her first house adequately describes this particular parent.

Moon, Ruler of the Ascendant, in the First House in Leo: With Leo on the second house cusp and the Moon in Leo in the first house, these individuals are far more ambitious than the average Cancerian. They have lofty ideas and expensive tastes. They want to be in positions in which they can rule or supervise others. These are very independent people who do not tolerate being bossed or having their freedom restricted. They should take care of their eyes, heart and back, and avoid stressful situations, as this is the ruler of the Cancer ascending sign. Children, either the native's own or those of others, will keep the environment active. This is not a particularly fruitful sign, and without good supportive aspects, especially from the Sun, Venus or Jupiter, may limit the amount of children or restrict them altogether.

Moon, Ruler of the Ascendant, in the Second House in Leo: These natives may walk with an upright carriage and wear their hair like the lion's mane, around the face and pulled down over the forehead. They can be generous to a fault, especially where the immediate family, children and romantic interests are concerned. All of these areas can be a source of financial drain from time to time and they must exercise restraint and draw the line with generosity. Goal oriented toward achieving financial security, they love luxurious things but won't put their savings or inner security in jeopardy. They have a great deal of obstinate pride and will not seek financial help until they are really down and out. They will, on occasion, brag about possession and the cost of the product under discussion.

Moon, Ruler of the Ascendant, in the Second House in Virgo: This adds height to the stature and a tummy later in life, as well as a neat appearance, clear complexion and thinner hair. More reserved than the average Cancerian, they are industrious, caring and sympathetic. This is an excellent placement for those who want to work in the medical field or in bookkeeping, secretarial, accounting or data processing, and they may work in credit unions or serve in the armed forces. They have good recall of childhood memories, sometimes to a fault, as they are apt to repeat many times over how relatives took advantage of them financially. An older woman, who could be a coworker, aunt, sister or other close relative, will have a positive or negative effect upon finances. They spend money on vitamins and health care products, and if they have pets, the care and medical treatment of them.

Moon, Ruler of the Ascendant, in the Third House in Virgo: These natives are taller and thinner, and may have a protruding tummy later in life. Because this is a changeable planet in a mutable sign in a mutable house, nervous stress could prevail, causing ulcers or gastric disturbances. Smoking should be avoided as the third house also governs the lungs. Very reserved, careful in speech and firm believers in education, they tend to carp on a subject and don't know when to let go. They may travel with someone met through work, at school or while attending a lecture. A sister of the mother may be considered an interfering person who tries to run the native's personal affairs, and an older woman, possibly a neighbor, is likely to call the police to report a noisy dog or children. The health concerns of an older neighbor could be of prime concern or require the care and services of these natives at some point in life.

Moon, Ruler of the Ascendant, in the Third House in Libra: These individuals love candy, cake and cookies, and will have to guard against obesity, especially later in life. Good looking, possibly with dimples in the cheeks or a cleft in the chin, they are light footed and can be good on the dance floor. They love to sing, but a talent for this is determined by the aspects to the Moon; a square from Venus, ruler of the sign position of the Moon's placement, will reduce the quality. Their congenial, sociable, amiable, generous and receptive mentality makes a good public relations person, a diplomat or a marriage or school counselor, as well as success in the creative arts. They love finery and jewelry. Peace and harmony in the immediate environment is a must to maintain balance within the system. There is the possibility of a partnership with an older woman; whether constructive or not depends upon the aspects to the Moon in the third house.

Moon, Ruler of the Ascendant, in the Fourth House in Libra: There are strong domestic ties, and these natives should be excellent at interior decorating, even on a limited budget. Sociable, friendly, generous and fond of pleasure and personal adornments, they love to entertain at home and make good hostesses. There may be a close bond or an emotional attachment to one of the parents, usually the mother. Men with this placement have to be careful of impressionable attachments, especially with married women. With either sex, a female may play a partnership role in connection with real estate, property or joint ownership of a multiple dwelling. This placement offers a greater chance of inheritance of property from a parent-in-law. The Moon in Libra in the fourth house often indicates activity surrounding the affairs of the mate's mother.

Moon, Ruler of the Ascendant, in the Fourth House in Scorpio: This placement of the Moon should blend well with Cancer rising as both are of the water element. The nature is responsive and sympathetic, with less sarcasm than ordinarily accompanies the Scorpio sign. There is too much fondness for pleasure, comfort and desire to satisfy the tastes, which can lead to weight problems. Chances are greater for inheritance or financial benefits. These natives should avoid undue stress in connection with family or travel that could react unfavorably on the health. High blood pressure can stem from a troubling marriage or family problems. The mother is apt to be a domineering, dictatorial type of parent.

Moon, Ruler of the Ascendant, in the Fifth House in Scorpio: Scorpio does not blend well with Leo's natural house. Men with this placement are apt to meet women who are demanding, dictatorial, critical and financially draining. These women always seem to want to change or redo something about the male's way of life, either their style of dress, personal habits or even their choice of associates. Women with this natal placement may have difficulty in conceiving, or surgery may be necessary with childbirth. This location can signify difficulties with the opposite sex and in the marriage state. It is not advisable to co-sign a mortgage agreement for a child or a romantic attachment as there is a likelihood of their failure to keep up the payments. Mutual funds, inheritance or an insurance settlement may also be tied in some way with matters concerning children or a love relationship. This can be a good placement for those who want to teach school children.

Moon, Ruler of the Ascendant, in the Fifth House in Sagittarius: A high forehead is a distinctive facial feature along with a clean, outdoor, sportsman look. This placement of the Moon does not blend well with Cancer rising as water and fire do not mix; it tends to add a little quirk in the nature. These natives have a good disposition and are generous but impetuous and passionate. They run the gamut from love of home to love of freedom and independence, and vacillate from wanting children to not having them, ever fearful of having to give up their desire for travel or pursue a college degree. The mother or mother-in-law may try to interfere with the rearing of children, even to the point of seeking legal guardianship, especially if the Moon makes a hard aspect to natal Jupiter. In a male's chart, women of foreign background or of vastly different backgrounds will enter the lives of these natives and whether these relationships produce positive or negative results depends on the aspects of the Moon and the condition of natal Jupiter, ruler of the Moon's sign position.

Moon, Ruler of the Ascendant, in the Sixth House in Sagittarius: Honest, kind and dependable, these natives are respected by their coworkers. They are not afraid of hard work but can get emotional at the first sign of a layoff, strike or anything that threatens their job security. Their place of employment is usually located in a county that is different from their own locality. Some may do a great deal of traveling or driving from one company office to another. Contacts with people from all walks of life and of other races and nationalities may be part of their work-related duties. One of my clients is a correction officer and has to deal with young people from a variety of backgrounds. Others work as airline reservationists, in the printing industry, driving city trucks or teaching adult education classes. Obesity and hip problems are the two areas for health concerns, and the mother or mother-in-law may have a minor health problem or disability. The health of an aunt who lives in a distant city may also be a source of worry. Or, it could be an aunt-in-law, someone on the mate's side of the family.

Moon, Ruler of the Ascendant in the Sixth House in Capricorn: This placement is apt to reflect on the health of the natives early in life through frequent colds and other chronic conditions. They have to take care of their teeth and skin as these areas are likely to pose a problem; there may be morbid and fanciful anxiety about health issues. These individuals may have to work the evening shift or have a female boss that is cold, aloof, reserved, unsympathetic and difficult to work with. They may have to take responsibility for and care for an older female, the mother, grandmother, aunt or other relative.

Moon, Ruler of the Ascendant, in the Seventh House in Capricorn: This placement brings the natives into intimate contact with the general public, but due to Capricorn, probably later in life or through political affiliations. These individuals are ambitious and have a desire to achieve personal recognition and esteem and, for status reasons, are more likely to own a briefcase than the average Cancerian. Cancerians seek marriage or business partners with similar tastes, needs and a sense of responsibility, and those who will exercise care and caution in money matters as well as being practical and hard working. With hard aspects to the Moon in Capricorn in the seventh house, Cancerians are likely to marry someone vastly different in age or one who may become cold, calculating and at times indifferent to the emotional needs and feelings of the native. Cancerians may be drawn to someone older or more mature because of past rejection by those of their own age group. Women with this placement are likely to attract women who are not in sympathy with them, and are more likely to be of benefit to their women friends than to receive benefits from them. Men with the Moon in Capricorn may be seeking a wife with qualities similar to the mother, and sometimes the wife turns into a nag, one who may become cold and unsympathetic. They will, however, be reliable and faithful, with a strong sense of moral responsibility. Depending on the aspects, these natives may join forces with a parent in a kind of partnership arrangement—for example, jointly purchasing rental property.

Moon, Ruler of the Ascendant, in the Seventh House in Aquarius: These Cancerians are advanced in their views and ideas, and have a great interest in working with organizations and group-related activities. They are broad-minded, intelligent and idealistic, with a friendly and courteous disposition. This is a favorable placement for public recognition and they are an asset to any club as a member of the public relations committee. These individuals can also be quite independent and somewhat unconventional, which can lead to trouble through female companions. The male wants a partner who dares to be different, unique in her own style of dress and who will do harmless, yet unconventional things on the spur of the moment. He also wants a mate who introduces new, interesting and exciting events into his life and is able to carry on an interesting conversation and yet be domesticated when the occasion calls for it. For either sex there is the possibility of going into partnership with an older female friend; whether this is advisable or not depends on the aspects the Moon makes with other planets.

Moon, Ruler of the Ascendant, in the Eighth House in Aquarius: This is not the best placement as Aquarius air does not blend well with the watery element of Scorpio's natural house. These individuals are very secretive about personal affairs and may be difficult to understand or communicate with, and may have a hard, somewhat cynical nature that reveals itself from time to time. There is a strong attraction to unusual and scientific studies, the occult and life in the hereafter. Should the Moon in Aquarius be in hard aspect with Pluto or planets in Scorpio, these natives may have an abnormal curiosity in the supernatural; if this goes unchecked they may at times dabble with black magic as a means of getting even with those they feel have done them an injustice. There is a good possibility of gain through an inheritance, property, mutual funds or a divorce settlement. As Aquarius rules catastrophe, this placement may bring about an insurance settlement through a mishap involving a large multiple dwelling or building that has several units, such as a hotel, condo or office building. Or, they could be victims of a national disaster that may or may not be covered by insurance, such as an earthquake, mud slide, flood or hurricane, or as a result of severe and sudden changes in weather conditions. Women with this placement may have miscarriages or abortions, or be unable to conceive due to unusual, prevailing conditions involving the female reproductive organs. With extremely hard aspects, it is possible that a parent may have sexually abused the native during the formative years.

Moon, Ruler of the Ascendant, in the Eighth House in Pisces: This placement governs that which is hidden beneath the surface and in the depths of the nature. Pisces is more compatible with Scorpio's natural house and these Cancerians are able to feel and sense if conditions are right for them. They desire material things and hold on tightly for sentiment's sake with the hope that someday they will be able to make good use of it. Highly emotional, romantic, sentimental and passionate, they are very receptive to surrounding conditions as this configuration increases the capacity for psychic and intuitive ability. They may undergo unusual experiences with ghosts or have contact with a departed member of the family, especially the mother or grandmother, and may experience psychic dreams or disturbing nightmares. These natives can be easily led and influenced, either sexually or financially. As a result, unscrupulous people may attempt to deceive them through get-rich-quick schemes that deplete their savings. There is the possibility of encountering deception or fraud through insurance settlements, inheritance or mutual funds. In a man's chart, sex may have to be curtailed due to the wife's ill health or her unstable mental condition. Women with this placement may have to forego sex due to the husband's medication to stabilize certain health conditions, which could interfere with his ability to "rise to the occasion."

Moon, Ruler of the Ascendant, in the Ninth House in Pisces: These individuals may not be religious in the orthodox sense, but more in the spiritual sense, often stating, "I don't need to go to church. God is within me, and it is how you live and treat people that will count in the end." These Cancerians would like nothing better than to be able to have a cottage near the lake as a sort of getaway from the harshness and reality of life. With a powerful and fruitful imagination that would be excellent for creative writing and journalism, they can be fluent speakers, teachers or composers. Should the Moon trine the Ascendant, this will enlarge the scope and spur the native into doing something great and unusual. There is an ability to express the emotions through intellectual channels, and they have a striking personality that is charming and gracious. This may reflect itself through art, music, dancing or photography. They need to be careful when traveling and eating unfamiliar foods and spices, and different water can poison the system. There may be an in-law that is an alcoholic, a drug abuser or requires medication to control a serious health problem. These natives should always be careful to read the fine print when signing legal or binding contracts as they could contain misleading information. There is the possibility of deception or hidden matters if they engage in lawsuits.

Moon, Ruler of the Ascendant, in the Ninth House in Aries: These individuals have a strong, opinionated mentality that simulates the mind to work quickly and without proper forethought. They can be so sure of themselves that they seldom take the time to listen to the advice or suggestions of others. Impulsive, self-reliant and independent, their driving force of energy projects itself onto others, draining the natives and leaving them feeling exhausted. Because of their short tempers, they undergo emotional flareups at the slightest provocation and say or do things they are certain to regret later. They are likely to pursue legal action against other parties because of accidents or mechanical defects in the home or commercial products that the manufacturer won't recognize. Men and women experience difficulty in getting along with bossy sisters-in-law or mothers-in-law. Men with this configuration are likely to meet female companions who are highly intelligent, passionate and self-reliant. Not too domesticated, they are apt to be ambitious and business oriented.

Moon, Ruler of the Ascendant, in the Tenth House in Aries: Should the Moon square the Ascendant, there may be emotional inhibition or lack of emotional sensitivity and affection from one of the parents. These natives require an occupation where they can be their own boss and where they have freedom of movement and decision making, as they will not tolerate a boss peeking around the corner observing their every move. They are likely to say, "I am an adult and expect to be treated like one. I know what my duties are and am capable of handling them." Impressions reach the minds of these natives at such a rapid pace that it is difficult for them to doubt their senses. As a result, they are so convinced of the accuracy of their thoughts that they react immediately without a second thought. They are so sure of themselves that when others make incorrect statements, they feel compelled to correct them immediately, even in the presence of others. These Cancerians must learn to control their fiery enthusiasm and refrain from any attempt to take charge of existing situations. An older woman may be instrumental in advancing the career; others, who may be jealous of such success, may attempt to tarnish the professional image.

Moon, Ruler of the Ascendant, in the Tenth House in Taurus: This is an excellent placement for the Moon as it is exalted in Taurus and comfortable in Capricorn's natural house. There is still the driving ambition to succeed in career or business, but these individuals go about it in a practical, cautious and reserved manner. Should the Moon sextile the Ascendant, the parents may have a comfortable income free from financial worries. This is good for those who are interested in working for the city, in politics, teaching and other occupations in which one is paid through city, state or federal taxes. These Cancerians gain esteem though their just, fair and honest nature, and are respected by their bosses and peers, usually rising to some position of authority or supervisory work. Women of wealth and influence play an important role in their quest for financial and business success. They should consider banking, real estate, hair styling or working in a restaurant as a hostess.

Moon, Ruler of the Ascendant, in the Eleventh House in Taurus: Hopes and wishes may be centered around financial security, family and owning a home free and clear. There is the likelihood of becoming involved with clubs and organizations, possibly even holding an officer's position such as treasurer. Older women of wealth and influence may be of financial assistance. Mothering friends, step-children or daughters- or sons-in-law is fine as long as they are not permitted to become a financial drain. It is also advisable to exercise caution if handling cash belonging to clubs or organizations to avoid the possible accusation of fund mismanagement.

Moon, Ruler of the Ascendant, in the Eleventh House in Gemini: These individuals are intellectual and could be clever writers. They have strong imaginations and ingenious, inventive, but somewhat changeable minds. There is a large circle of acquaintances but some may not be reliable. Short trips may be undertaken, as well as much letter writing and communication in general regarding a female companion. As the eleventh house is the ninth of the third, and with the Moon in Gemini, this is usually indicative of a sibling living in a distant city, requiring visits, letters and phone calls.

Moon, Ruler of the Ascendant, in the Twelfth House in Gemini: An imaginative mentality that may not see things as they really are is combined with a gentle, charming personality with compassion and understanding of humanity. With a changeable nature that is fond of diversity, there may be more than one outlet for creative interests. These individuals may be spiritual and mediumistic with a strong interest in psychism and the occult. This placement endows a certain flair to body movements and a manner of speaking that is likely to hold the attention of others. Thus, they make excellent spellbinding speakers. Many love large animals, especially horses. Gemini can be ultra-romantic and impressionable and easily led into acts of indiscretion through overly stimulating the imagination; this often leads to emotional flirtations. They may benefit more by working behind the scenes in occupations requiring quiet solitude than with the public at large, and may discover they do their best work in creative writing or other mental pursuits if done in isolated surroundings. There may be secrets regarding a sibling, or they may have mental or emotional problems, or a learning disability.

Moon, Ruler of the Ascendant in the Twelfth House in Cancer: Emotions predominate over logic and an overly imaginative mind can get out of hand and lead to acts of indiscretion. They may have unusual tastes in food, and experience an emotional inhibition or experience lack of affection through one of the parents. Very receptive to surroundings.

Leo Ascendant

Fixed   Fire
Positive   Ruler: Sun.

Leo is the Sun-ruled sign of the natural fifth house with emphasis on romance, children, games of chance, all places of amusement and entertainment, schools, sporting events and creative talents or hobbies.

Character Traits

Leo's generosity and faith in humanity can be a handicap in blinding them to the faults of their friends or romantic interests because they have complete trust in others. This often makes them poor judges of character.

They don't mind if you borrow anything that belongs to them as long as you put it back exactly where you found it, not where you think it belongs.

Natural born leaders, they like to be boss and delegate orders, and their secret desire is to hold a management position.

Leos need to be loved, admired and told they are wonderful; flattery builds up the ego and helps them feel better about themselves.

When Leos brag and beat their own drums, it is to cover up a lack of self-confidence and self-esteem. By bragging and calling attention to their priceless possessions or their accomplishments, they are attempting to uplift their image and appear important. The more a Leo brags, the more evidence there is that points to lack of parental approval and support. In a majority of cases, it was the father, who may have been a good, hard working parent but never gave the Leo child praise and approval; or there was a lack of communication between the two of them.

Fixed signs are goal oriented people and when Leos set their sights on a particular course of action it is difficult to sway them in a different direction. Their staying power enables them to stick with a project until it is finished. This can be a disadvantage with relationships, refusing to let go even when they realize it is over. However, once they do make up their minds to end a relationship, they do so without a backward glance and will have nothing further to do with that person once the decision has been made.

They can suffer deep moods of deression from emotional or financial setbacks which result from unwise choices in friends or personal relationships, but their faith in mankind is so strong they are ready to forgive and forget. They are endowed with much optimism and a deep sense of pride in their accomplishments, and are especially happy when others take notice of them.

As a rule, Leos are affectionate, loving, generous and easygoing individuals with a real zest for living. They are fun to have around as their free-spirited enthusiasm can be quite catchy. They have a great flair for the dramatic, and at times can be overbearing domineering and arrogant.

Although they are generous, it has to be given freely and willingly on their own. Should someone try to push them into donating or lending money, Leos will balk and outright refuse.

They have good organizational ability and a way of exercising constructive authority in the handling of others under their command. It is for this reason they make good military people. Their charm and flair for the dramatic is great for acting and entertainment, and their magnetic personality may even draw some into a political career where they can shine before the public. But a supervisory or management position is likely to be their first choice of occupation.

Physical Appearance

Individuals possess some of the Leo qualities and physical features if they have any of the following configurations in the natal chart:
- Leo rising
- Sun in the first house
- Sun within orb of aspect with the Ascendant's degree
- Ruler of the first house cusp in Leo
- Ruler of the first house conjunct or otherwise in close aspect with the Sun
- Sun or Moon in Leo
- Moon in close aspect with the Sun
- Leo intercepted in the first house

Leo rising individuals possess one or more of the following features:

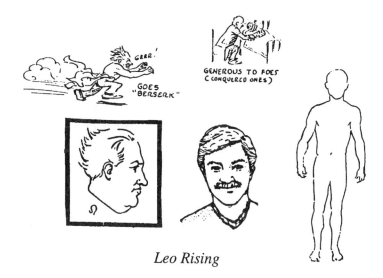

Leo Rising

- Receding hairline in later life, which they try to conceal by drawing some of the hair forward across the head, somewhat like a lion's mane
- Often bony, prominent knees, narrow hips and an upright carriage
- Thin upper lip, which males disguise with a mustache
- One eyebrow may be higher than the other
- Some wear eyeglasses to correct defective vision
- Average height, broad shoulders with upper torso larger than lower half
- Full neck, but longer than that of a Taurus rising individual
- Hair sometime grows low and heavy on the back of the neck; men often have this area shaved
- Flat bridge on the upper part of the nose (like a cat's nose), which makes it difficult to wear glasses

Mentality

Clue Words: Impulsive, dramatic, temperamental, purposeful, trustworthy

The Leo mind has a strong dislike of details, preferring to leave that job for others. They are good at dispatching unpleasant tasks or duties to someone else, and only do well with subjects that are of interest to them. Anything outside this range is treated with much indifference. Stubborn and fixed in opinions, it is difficult to get them to change their minds once they are made up. They are likely to have a dramatic flair in speech, actions and presentation, and are gentle when unprovoked, but formidable when angry. They are honest, loyal and faithful.

Romantic Inclinations

Clue Words: Ardent, dominant, charming, possessive, affectionate, considerate

They can be generous to a fault if their partners continue to tell them on a daily basis that they are terrific, wonderful, considerate, adorable and marvelous lovers. Leos need to feel they are loved and appreciated. Every lion needs a mate, and this is even more true with a Leo because they cannot function internally without someone to love who loves them in return.

Health

Leo governs the arteries, back, eyes, heart and circulatory system; cataracts or glaucoma, lazy eye and eye problems in general, left eye of the female and right eye of the male; strokes and heart ailments; spine and spinal column; the constitution and recuperative powers; and fevers, inflammation, sunburn and sunstroke

Ascendant Ruler in Signs and Houses

Sun, Ruler of the Ascendant, in the First House in Leo: Whenever the ruler of the Ascendant is in the first house, it emphasizes the motivational influence of the sign. Ruler Sun in Leo adds more determination and fixity to the nature of these independent individuals who may politely listen to suggestions and then do it their own way. They have good organizational ability, and love power and authority. The nature is strong and forcible with great vitality. Lovers of the opposite sex, music, dancing, recreation, sports and games such as chess, tennis, golf and racquetball, they usually maintain a youthful appearance as they grow older. They are dignified, just and loyal, and may walk with an upright carriage to ease a sensitive back problem. Ambitious, reliable and dependable, they are enthusiastic and love action when they have the opportunity to lead or influence others and delegate projects. Their secret desire is to hold a supervisory or management position, but they dislike anything mean or underhanded. In a woman's chart, with soft aspects, the father, husband, children, lover or men in general will be of beneficial assistance in promoting their self-centered interests. In a male's chart, the father, children and men in authority will assist them in some favorable way. In either sex, with hard aspects, there is low resistance when recuperating from an illness, and men and children may be a source of friction. They should watch their eyes, heart and back for possible health problems.

Sun, Ruler of the Ascendant in the First House in Virgo: Energetic, practical and stable, with the ability to put ideas to concrete and material use, these conservative, reserved individuals are industrious and persevere in the fulfillment of duties. They are neat and careful in appearance, orderly, critical and dependent on others. They may develop a tummy in later years because Virgo rules the abdomen. The father, husband or boss may be hyper-critical, demanding and faultfinding. Since the first house is the eighth of the sixth, an aunt or uncle may have problems with the heart, circulatory system, back or eyes. Or, in some way, the aunt or uncle may play a more important role in the Leo's life. This is a good placement for those who want to work in the health or medical field.

Sun, Ruler of the Ascendant, in the Second House in Virgo: There is a good deal of shrewdness and a strong desire for money. Vocational duties may require keeping records of work schedules, time sheets or personal funds spent on travel, products or services rendered. Gain is likely through the influence and support of men in positions of authority. Money may be obtained through practical and industrious efforts and financial assistance is possible through the father or an uncle. This placement is a strong indication that at some time in life they are apt to receive benefits through the government by working in the armed forces or government, or receiving unemployment benefits, sick benefits or Worker's Compensation.

Sun, Ruler of the Ascendant, in the Second House in Libra: Quality is number one with these individuals, who will never be happy with hand-me-downs or inferior goods. They are likely to have good taste in clothing and accessories and may spend too much on luxury items. Women with this placement and soft aspects are likely to gain through their husband or a romantic interest who is likely to give them frequent gifts and flowers. There is the likelihood of gain through men on the partner's side of the family. In a man's chart, give careful consideration to the condition of the seventh house and natal Venus before going into a financial arrangement with a partner. With hard aspects, especially from Saturn Uranus, Pluto or Neptune, the natives can suffer financial loss. In some cases, they may have to attend social affairs as a means of making new business contacts to increase income. If the Sun in Libra receives hard aspects, female Leos may lack ambition and depend solely on the resources of others or the marriage partner for their income.

Sun, Ruler of the Ascendant, in the Third House in Libra: The mind is resourceful, creative and ambitious, and Libra instills a strong desire to achieve recognition and distinction through intellectual accomplishments. They have the ability to see both sides of an issue and will carefully weigh the pros and cons before reaching a decision. In a confrontation that requires resolution of a problem, they apply finesse and graciousness of manner with a willingness to meet the other person half way. However, if they are unable to arrive at a workable solution, they take their "white gloves" off and in a warlike fashion exercise force that no one expects. The Sun in Libra in the third house tends to attract people and things who can further the Leo rising's interests. There are strong indications that they, or their marriage partners, may go into partnership with a sibling, not necessarily in business but perhaps through a mutual creative enterprise. Before a Leo goes into partnership with a sibling, these factors should be checked: the seventh house (natural house of partners) and its ruler, the condition of Venus (ruler of the Sun sign) and Mercury (natural ruler of the third house of siblings), not only in the natal chart, but for any recent eclipses or major transits that may be activating any of these planets. Generally, when someone speaks of going into a partnership, there is always more than one major transit or a recent eclipse that will highlight these interests.

Sun, Ruler of the Ascendant, in the Third House in Scorpio: When the Ascendant sign and its ruler are in fixed signs, there is a marked degree of persistence and stubborn adherence to personal views and ideas. There is strong willpower with the emotions being stabilized by the intellect. The nature is commanding, frank and outspoken, and if the Sun squares the Ascendant's degree, they can be somewhat sarcastic, cutting and abrupt in speech. These Leos possess probing minds that love challenging games of strategy such as chess, crossword puzzles or computer games. Short trips and mass mailings could be financially productive through a product or service handled through the mail. There is financial gain or loss through men in connection with mutual funds, inheritance or an insurance settlement. These Leos are likely to outlive their siblings, and one brother or sister may have a serious heart condition or problems with high blood pressure. (Before passing judgment on the possible loss of a sibling, it is important to check the condition of natal Pluto, ruler of the Sun's sign position, natal Mercury, the house containing Gemini and also the ruler of the eighth house and planets therein.) This is an excellent placement for a researcher, troubleshooter, insurance agent, stockbroker or anyone who works with death certificates or funeral parlors and matters of the dead.

Sun, Ruler of the Ascendant, in the Fourth House in Scorpio: This intensifies all interests of a domestic nature and concerns about family interests. As the fourth house governs the early years, a parent, generally the father, played a major role in the molding of the Leo's character traits. If there are hard aspects to the Sun in Scorpio in the fourth house from planets in the first house, the father may have passed away early in life or was an extremely demanding, dictatorial parent who demanded perfection. Sometimes the Scorpio parent may attempt to force the Leo child into a profession that is totally alien to the Leo, or it may be that nothing the child attempts is good enough to satisfy the parent. An inferiority complex or a lack of self-worth may be instilled through this harsh parental influence. With soft aspects the influence of the father is especially marked with a strong bond of affection. This placement often produces an inheritance or property gain through parents. Men with hard aspects to the Sun in the fourth house may lose their home or property through a divorce settlement or as a result of child support. Much depends on the aspects to the natal Sun, Pluto and Moon (natural ruler of the fourth house) and the condition of the eighth hosue of inheritance (note the ruler of the eighth house and planets therein). The later years should be more productive than the early ones with a chance of honor and recognition in declining years. Some Leos with this placement may at some point own income property. Transits to the Sun in the fourth house will indicate when problems are likely to arise through tenants.

Sun, Ruler of the Ascendant, in the Fourth House in Sagittarius: There is much pride and self-confidence with the ability to influence others through logic, philosophy and abstract thought. These are warm, helpful, sincere, friendly individuals who give freely of their time and energy. More demonstrative than the average Leo, at the same time they are more likely to rebel against those who may attempt to restrict their freedom and independent spirit. They may not be interested in traveling unless it is necessary for intellectual gratification or to enhance career prospects. These Leos have more driving power, and are considered more talkative but not quite so naive. The father is instrumental in the positive unfolding of the character, and the parents are likely to own more than once piece of property (perhaps a dual dwelling for extra income purposes). Others may own a trailer in an out of the way place and use it for weekend getaways. With hard aspects to the Sun, they may have problems with future in-laws, especially the father-in-law, who may not approve of the relationship due to a vast difference in cultural background or religious beliefs.

Sun, Ruler of the Ascendant, in the Fifth House in Sagittarius: There is no better protection than to have the Sun in its own house and also in the comfortable sign of Sagittarius. These individuals are interested in sports, pleasurable pursuits, computer games, golf, tennis, racquetball, chess and games in general. They are romantically attracted to those of different backgrounds, intellectual levels, religions and cultures. With hard aspects, there is a strong possibility that these Leos may lose the object of their affections through forced relocation. In a male's chart, it could be the girlfriend's family moving away, or the Leo is transferred to another state and the girlfriend is unable to join him. Because Sagittarius has legal connotations, it is possible that a child may become involved with questionable characters and get into trouble with the police department. One of the children is certain to move to a distant city for temporary reasons during service in the armed forces, while attending college or living with distant relatives during summer vacation.

Sun, Ruler of the Ascendant, in the Fifth House in Capricorn: These natives lack sympathy and may have false pride. They are overly conservative but good workers with good organizational ability and want to rise to positions of authority. Attracted to those in a different age group or of a mature disposition, romantic partners may be widows or widowers, and most likely already parents by previous marriages. They are likely to experience disillusionment through love affairs or rejection thereof, which may account for their interest in older people. This placement may limit the number of children as Leos may regard them as a heavy responsibility that restricts personal freedom.

Sun, Ruler of the Ascendant, in the Sixth House in Capricorn: These individuals are likely to resent limitations or restrictions imposed on them if they are forced to conform with circumstances in the workplace. They can easily become depressed and will be slower in making friends. Timidity may result in a decrease in self-reliance, and they can be distrustful of others, cold, reserved and austere. The father or a child may have chronic health problems. With soft aspects, there is a strong desire to be of service to humanity, and a desire for importance is gained through hard work and benefits derived from laborious efforts. The natives take responsibility seriously and are not afraid of hard work; they may have to work the evening shift at some time. Lacking vitality and tiring easily, the health of these individuals may not be the best during early years, with frequent colds and other classic childhood ailments. They may be susceptible to teeth problems, skin disorders, knee ailments, rheumatism or injuries through work. There may be a lack of appreciation for their efforts on the part of bosses and those in authority. This is a good placement for government jobs, civil service, health and welfare.

Sun, Ruler of the Ascendant, in the Sixth House in Aquarius: This placement denotes unusual talents, perception, independence, originality and enterprise. There is success through working with the government, computers, electronics, aeronautics and group-related activities or organizations and associations. These individuals dislike boring routine work, preferring variety and doing something tomorrow that's different from what they did today. Adverse to conventional occupations and in need of a job where there is freedom of movement and independence in thought and action, these individuals cannot tolerate jobs where they stand in one place all day, pulling the same lever over and over. They can be rebel against those in authority, and have a tendency to be scientific in thought with a love of research. There is persistence in choosing their own course of action, whether right or wrong, as they want to make their own way in life and do not like conventional or routine occupations. They may have deep rooted and obscure ailments that may be difficult to cure. Women with this placement may have difficulty becoming pregnant or experience trouble during pregnancy or delivery. This sometimes indicates a miscarriage or an abortion. They are likely to come in contact with unusual people, astrologers, eccentrics or borderline geniuses through the place of employment.

Sun, Ruler of the Ascendant, in the Seventh House in Aquarius: The seventh house indicates the type of people these natives will attract from time to time. Leos with this placement are likely to attract proud, successful, warm hearted, friendly and unusual people or partners. Success may depend on the Leo's willingness to work with others. In a male's chart, partnerships may be formed with friends, friends may help the Leo rise to a higher social position through contacts with business people and superiors. This is an excellent placement for astrological counseling and working with clubs or organizations. In a female's chart, the likelihood is great for marrying someone with an unusual sense of humor, who is a bit eccentric but interesting, and who will need personal freedom to mingle and get together with friends. Leos usually have a great deal of sympathy and devotion for causes. With hard aspects in a male's chart, there is likely to be opposition from men in authority and tough competition from others in similar fields. It is good for the formation of close bonds between friends, companionship and business or marriage partnerships. Cooperative efforts are needed between the native and others, whether in public, family or brotherhood. Females with hard aspects may experience divorce or separation, or the partner may experience unexpected and sudden health upsets involving the heart, back or other deep-rooted conditions.

Sun, Ruler of the Ascendant, in the Seventh House in Pisces: These Leos usually have a strong imagination, vision, ideals and aims. They can be inspirational in speaking, writing, music or the creative arts, and can easily tune in to the public needs. There is charm and magnetism, with good intuition. This is a good placement for those who want to operate a bar, be musicians, artists, detectives or work with boats. They have to be careful when business partnerships do not carry their own weight. If Leos feel they are doing all the work, they may eventually seek legal counsel for the best way to end the relationship. Females with hard aspects to the Sun may marry someone who abuses drugs or alcohol, is deceptive or about whom there is some kind of mystery or strange or secretive circumstance. Both men and women have to be careful of gullibility and manipulation through others.

Sun, Ruler of the Ascendant, in the Eighth House in Pisces: Wills, insurance policies, inheritance, family trusts and mutual funds or joint ownership of property or possessions need clearly defined paperwork to avoid the possibility of confusion or complications involving the settlement of these issues. These Leos may be easily influenced or led regarding finances, and are apt to be overly generous and extravagant. When the natal Sun is in the eighth house, they should exercise caution around the forty-fourth to forty-sixth years of life. The progressed Sun will begin to approach a semisquare aspect (forty-five degrees) to the natal Sun in the eighth house at age forty-four and will be exact at forty-five, leaving the aspect at forty-six. During this period of time, they should carefully note the major transits to the Sun, natal or progressed, the ruler of the natal or progressed eighth house cusp and eclipses that may highlight important configurations in the natal or progressed chart. This is especially important because the Sun is also the ruler of the ascending sign. Females tend to gain financially after marriage as the eighth house is the second of the seventh house. Medication (Sun in Pisces) should be taken exactly as prescribed by a physician, especially if it is for minor heart ailments. In a female's chart, the prescribed medication for her husband's health problem may interfere with his ability to "rise to the occasion." If such is the case, the husband should contact the physician for a possible change of prescription. The Sun in the eighth house can indicate a long life, but because it is placed in Pisces these individuals must adhere to realistic virtues and avoid abuse of drugs, alcohol, food and sex. Surgery on the feet may be necessary for removal of warts or bunions.

Sun, Ruler of the Ascendant, in the Eighth House in Aries: Leos usually have red hair or a reddish glint to the hair, a ruddy complexion and possibly a scar, mole or mark on the face. They can be more aggressive, assertive, dynamic, passionate and fun loving than the average Leo, and may have discovered sex early in youth. Money through the resources of others plays a dominant role, and they may join forces with another male in a mutual financial enterprise. There is the possibility that a male member of the family will be injured in a violent accident. For some Leos, surgery on the face or jaw line for removal of a cyst or tumor may be necessary at some point in life.

Sun, Ruler of the Ascendant, in the Ninth House in Aries: Self-reliant and confident, these people are independent thinkers who defend their beliefs in the face of all odds. Travel is likely, but the Arian quality may tie in with the armed forces, education, camping or sporting events such as the Indianapolis 500. Lawsuits may occur in connection with accidents, mechanical defects in a product that the manufacturer won't back up or a personal affront or personal liability. A brother- or sister-in-law may be accident prone or have a scar, mole or mark on the head or face. Women with this configuration may marry someone of a different background or social or intellectual level. A grandchild may also be accident prone or suffer a head injury, especially if it is a boy or an athletic, independent and difficult to control girl.

Sun, Ruler of the Ascendant, in the Ninth House in Taurus: The bodies of these natives are physically strong and well-proportioned, and they are conservative with reserved and careful manners. They have the ability to concentrate, and are slow to anger but explosive when pushed. Their thinking is calm and rational and they are extremely patient, fiercely defending their ideas, which are seldom abandoned; this is because it is not always easy for them to make or accept changes or to adapt themselves to new lines of thought and action. While others consider these Leos to be extremely stubborn and slow in making up their minds, in reality they are trying to assimilate and weigh the facts carefully before arriving at a concrete decision. Expense-paid travel may be a part of occupational duties. Sometimes a retraining program or an additional college course may be necessary, perhaps due to new equipment or the introduction of new techniques; the company is likely to pay the tuition. Women with this configuration are apt to marry someone (or have a brother-in-law), who earns income through teaching, publishing, travel or the religious life. A brother-in-law may be of financial assistance or the cause of finanical loss, and these natives may be designated legal guardians for the estate of a grandchild.

Sun, Ruler of the Ascendant, in the Tenth House in Taurus: There is a great sense of dignity and a love for exercising power and authority. These Leos are certain to reach positions of importance. The hard aspects do not deny success; they only hinder or place a few stumbling blocks in the path. Sometimes these restrictions help build strength of character and appreciation for what the natives have achieved as they have to work harder to get there than others in the same category. With soft aspects, there is sound judgment with strong common sense. These individuals have practical, conscientious ability for executive and management positions, and the configurations instill ambition, strength of will and excellent organizational ability. Men of influence, authority and wealth may be of benefit. Money and company benefits will be given first and foremost consideration when seeking employment.

Sun, Ruler of the Ascendant, in the Tenth House in Gemini: There is a strong desire to achieve distinction through intellectual accomplishments, and these natives are eager to investigate new things and teach new lines of thought in connection with their occupation. The mind is resourceful, creative and ambitious for success and honor through mental efforts. There is the desire to uplift, enlighten and assist others mentally. Frequent short trips, phone calls, letters, paperwork and other forms of communication may be connected with their duties. With hard aspects to the Sun in Gemini in the tenth house, these Leos can be intellectual snobs or display arrogance to those of a lesser educational level. Many follow in the career footsteps of the father, sibling or other family member, and they are likely to hold more than one job at a time, perhaps a full-time occupation with a lucrative sideline. This is a good placement for teachers, secretaries, data processors, the communications field or any occupation where knowledge is transmitted or the ability to handle several duties at one time is a necessity.

Sun, Ruler of the Ascendant, in the Eleventh House in Gemini: These individuals have the ability to express themselves through unique and unusual fields or occupations that are connected with teaching, writing, lecturing or transmitting knowledge. Hopes and wishes may be centered around writing, teaching or published material, and they have inventive, inquisitive minds interested in astrology or the occult sciences. Friends and acquaintance are usually met through school, travel or clubs and organizations. These Leos love to debate and may even take the opposite viewpoint just for the sake of a friendly argument. Travel may be in connection with tour groups or to attend seminars to enhance and learn new techniques. They are dualistic and likely to join or belong to more than one association. A sibling may move to a distant city as the eleventh house is the ninth house of the third house, and with Gemini on the eleventh house cusp or a planet in Gemini therein, it generally indicates either legal matters surrounding the affairs of a sibling or moving to a distant city. With hard aspects to the Sun in Gemini, Leos may not be able to depend too much on their friends as some are likely to be unreliable.

Sun, Ruler of the Ascendant, in the Eleventh House in Cancer: The ego goes through periods of emotional flareups and fear or rejection holds them back from establishing close ties. They may play a parental role to friends to achieve a bond of affection. Some seek friends who are mature or older because they feel safer emotionally with them. They are attracted to unusual individuals. These Leos appear to be self-sufficient, but deep inside they are terribly sensitive, emotional and adverse to criticism of any kind. They are likely to have step-children, but much depends on the aspects to the Sun. Club activities may be associated with family, such as Parents Without Partners or Weight Watchers. Sometimes Leos share the same friends as those of family members, who may be instrumental in the introduction of these acquaintances.

Sun, Ruler of the Ascendant, in the Twelfth House in Cancer: These individuals are secretive, emotionally sensitive and easily affected by environmental conditions. Men with this placement can be easily aroused through sympathy, but when it involves a family member, this display of sensitivity may be the result of a guilt complex rather than a sense of duty. They can make progress and be successful in life, but only if done so behind the scenes in a quiet, unobtrusive manner. They have good psychic and intuitive ability and may even consider teaching a course in the subject. In a female's chart, this configuration often indicates a husband who may resent any form of freedom or display of independence on the part of the Leo female, with a desire to keep her at home attending to his and the family's needs. If either men or women have emotional inhibitions, they could stem through parental relationships, usually the father, who may be detached, non-communicative or unresponsive in matters of love and affection. Because the twelfth house governs substitutes, in some case there may be a stepfather who may not display affection.

Sun, Ruler of the Ascendant, in the Twelfth House in Leo: With soft aspects to the Sun in the twelfth house, these individuals like plenty of company, to mix in society and entertain. Hospitable and generous in nature, they love water, can be good swimmers and have a desire to own a boat. They can succeed in the management field if duties keep them behind the scenes rather than in the public's eye. There is success in employment that deals with hospitals, institutions, jails, places of confinement and the armed forces, where they are likely to be stationed at lonely, isolated bases. With hard aspects to the Sun in Leo in the twelfth house, there can be self-imposed states of loneliness or separation from others due to a deflated ego from romantic rejection. In extreme cases, some Leo males may seek romantic involvement with their own sex. Women with hard aspects to the Leo Sun in the twelfth house may have hidden secrets regarding a child or the birth of a child, or a child may require temporary confinement due to mental or emotional disturbances. Adopted or step-children are also covered under such a configuration. There are clandestine affairs that seldom culminate in marriage.

Virgo Ascendant

Mutable   Earth
Negative   Ruler: Mercury.

Virgo is the Mercury-ruled sign of the natural sixth house, which governs matters concerning detail work, health and service to others. For this reason it is natural for Virgos to be interested in the medical field, real estate and occupations that require conscientious attention to details.

Character Traits

Virgo is on the cusp of the sixth house in the natural zodiac and represents logic and painstaking orderliness in the handling of everyday routines. The main characteristic of the Virgo nature is its marvelous creative talent, which can be either manual, such as flower arranging, or mental, such as writing articles and short stories.

Being an earth sign, Virgo is industrious, practical, reliable and responsible. Work is very important to these natives and they take great pains when handling even the smallest of details. With Mercury as the ruling planet, they are fond of learning, and may have an ingenious mind, albeit somewhat indecisive at times. They are critical and precise. Speaking ability is good, but they often go into too much repetition and detail.

Because Virgo is a mutable sign, they are adaptable and can adjust to new and different situations. They are well known for their analytical abilities. Their judgment is usually quite accurate, but they should avoid the tendency to be too judgmental or critical of themselves and others.

Extremely particular about hygiene, they try to take good care of their health through proper diet and exercise, but can be hypochondriacs, worrying too much about their health. Every little pain or symptom is sometimes stressed out of proportion.

Virgos are inclined to be quiet, aloof and reserved at first meeting, but quite talkative with good friends. They often find themselves in the capacity of serving or caring for others, and it is for this reason they make good healers, nurses, doctors, medical technicians and dieticians.

Many a Virgo has been referred to as a chronic faultfinder, when actually they are just as critical of themselves, or even more so, than they are of others. And, many a Virgo has been known to say, "But I was only trying to help," after being rebuffed by a friend or relative for making some small criticism against manners or way of dress. Actually, this is the Virgo's true intention for they do try hard to be helpful and are even baffled when their constructive advice, criticism or suggestions are not warmly received.

The one major fault of Virgo natives is their tendency to become overly lost in details. The homemaker may be so exacting and neat about housework that every minute is spent keeping order to the point of excluding contact with friends and social affairs. And others can do the same with business. Virgos are generally conservative, intelligent and cautious with an excellent capacity for gathering and interpreting knowledge and material. Because of this ability they do very well in the literary and scientific fields, where accuracy in details is a must. They also make excellent critics, teachers, bookkeepers, secretaries and data processors.

Physical Appearance

Individuals possess some Virgo qualities and physical features if they have any of the following configurations in the natal chart:
- Virgo rising
- Mercury in the first house, regardless of sign position
- Mercury within orb of aspect of the Ascendant's degree
- Ruler of the first house cusp in Virgo
- Ruler of the first house cusp conjunct or in another close aspect with Mercury
- Sun or Moon in Virgo
- Sun or Moon in close aspect with Mercury
- Virgo intercepted in the first house

Virgo rising individuals possess one or more of the following features:
- High forehead, long neck, long head
- Thin lips; face seldom becomes fleshy
- May get a tummy later in life as Virgo rules the abdomen
- Hair thins in later years but still covers the scalp

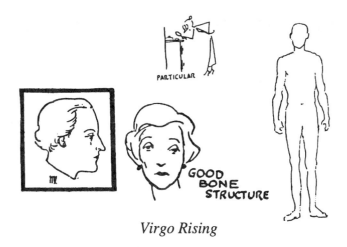

Virgo Rising

- Features are usually small, but nicely configured
- Sometimes the nose is slightly hooked
- Long body and arms give the impression of being taller
- Sometimes the head is tilted to one side when talking or listening
- Quiet voice, active walk with toes sometimes turned in

Mentality

Clue Words: Methodical, discriminating, critical, conservative, intelligent

The Virgo mind is orderly, dependable, secretive and reserved. They tend to worry about their health and sometimes are fussy about insignificant things. These individuals work well alone after they have been shown their duties, and prefer to go unnoticed. They are often dependent on others, yet want to be in the position to rule them. There is perseverance, but no real determination or ambition. They dislike physical work, and do best working alone in an orderly manner. Confusion and constant interruptions can easily upset their state of mind.

Romantic Inclinations

Clue Words: Careful, selective, shy, faithful, undemonstrative

Virgo natives are drawn to the opposite sex according to neatness, hygiene, mannerism and educational background. Some consider Virgo a prudish sign but once they find their true love, they can be the most passionate of all signs.

Health

The average Virgo remains more youthful in appearance for a longer period of time. Even when they are ill they look good. This could be due to their habit of watching their diet and food intake, and they generally know which foods are good for them and avoid the rest. Some take vitamin supplements, and Virgos are more knowledgeable about these matters than any other sign.

Virgo governs the abdominal region, the bowel and bowel disorders; the digestive tract and indigestion; the intestines and its disorders; mental stress, which reacts on the stomach, causing acidity, colitis, constipation or diarrhea; nervous illness and ulcers; skin conditions and psoriasis

Ascendant Ruler in Signs and Houses

Because Mercury is a sexless, neutral planet, it depends on aspects with other planets to give it motivation.

Mercury in aspect with the Sun: may gain or lose comprehension ability; Mercury in aspect with the Moon: mentality is conditioned by the emotions and psyche; Mercury in aspect with Venus: social and the tendency to balance situations; Mercury in aspect with Mars: adds energy to the mentality, quick wit and thinking; Mercury in aspect with Jupiter: sound judgment or the lack thereof; Mercury in aspect with Saturn: ability to concentrate, depth of thinking or depression; Mercury in aspect with Uranus: intensifies the intellect; genius or eccentric; Mercury in aspect with Neptune: receptivity, adaptability or chaos and confusion; Mercury in aspect with Pluto: perceptive or underhanded

Mercury, Ruler of the Ascendant, in the First House in Virgo: Mercury in the first house has the tendency to stimulate the mind and increase restlessness in the nature. There is an urge for direct contact, to talk and communicate with others, but these individuals should think before they act and learn to express themselves clearly and distinctively to avoid being misunderstood or misinterpreted. They have a nervous disposition and a changeable nature. Some are inclined to verbosity, which others find annoying, and they worry about insignificant things. Their minds are adaptable and inquiring, always in search of new information. Quick in speech, thought and action, they can jump to conclusions at times. With hard aspects it will not be easy to direct the thought and activities to preconceived ideas. Quick witted and quick with retorts, they are prone to exaggeration or sarcasm. An aunt or uncle plays a more active role than is ordinary. This is not a fruitful sign or planet, and is likely to limit brothers and sisters (or none at all).

Mercury, Ruler of the Ascendant, in the First House in Libra: These individuals are moderately tall and slender with a well-formed body. Sometimes they have dimples in their cheeks or a little cleft in the chin. Gracious, kind and charming, they must know and understand everything before they can become involved. The mind is creative and ingenious, and learns things easily. These individuals like to color-code things they work with such as file folders of different colors and, if possible, to have a color scheme for their work equipment. Color and pleasant working surroundings are a must if they are to function properly. Some like soft music playing while they work, but others find it annoying. They are systematic in their study of detail, careful of health and somewhat nervous in disposition. This is a good placement for writers, teachers, secretaries, lecturers, medical personnel and just about any occupation where it is necessary to be well organized, exacting and analytical. They love pets and especially canaries that sing to them. These natives work better in a teamwork situation or in public relations, and dislike hard, physical, dirty work. They are fortunate in acquiring property, but there is an inclination to domestic disputes with siblings on the marriage partner's side of the family.

Mercury, Ruler of the Ascendant, in the Second House in Libra: Usually patient, considerate and careful in speech, these individuals have good business sense that aids personal finances. The tendency is to give each purchase careful consideration, but even then they find it difficult to arrive at a decision as to what to buy. Sometimes they buy both items to avoid the necessity of making up their minds. They may socialize in connection with or to enhance earning potential, and may be collectors of books who prefer hardbound editions. Brothers- or sisters-in-law can be a source of financial gain or drain, and money can be obtained through literary or artistic pursuits or through marriage and business partnerships. Gain is possible through travel, communications and ordinary business and commercial affairs in general.

Mercury, Ruler of the Ascendant, in the Second House in Scorpio: There is a great deal of mental resourcefulness which is backed up by enough courage to force action and success in areas concerning finances. Their remarkably clear foresight and vision enables these Virgos to detect deception because they are swift to sense another person's motives. Invariably this position brings them in contact with conditions associated with the death of other people. They may be executors or experience difficulty through relatives who may be questioning the disposition of an estate. At various times they may have to deal with home, life or auto insurance agents, and it is wise for them to keep all personal and business income receipts and papers in a safe place as there is a likelihood of being audited by the IRS. These Virgos are more secretive than others concerning finances and are likely to have a way of earning money on the side that is kept secret for income tax purposes. They may receive checks in the mail through unemployment,

Social Security, Workers's Compensation or royalties for books or published material. As this is the sixth house of health of the ninth house of grandchildren and brothers- and sisters-in-law, there may be mental anguish concerning their health or surgery. With hard aspects there is a strong possibility of the loss of an inheritance or an insurance settlement through the intervention of a sibling. Sometimes this denotes the possibility of having to handle the estate of a deceased sibling. This placement is good for occupations dealing with mutual funds, payroll, scheduling of time sheets, working for the unemployment department or in the medical field, or for insurance agents, liquor agents, tax preparers and sex therapists.

Mercury, Ruler of the Ascendant, in the Third House in Scorpio: These Virgos have shrewd, secretive, penetrating minds that love to probe into deep research, especially in matters concerning astrology, metaphysics, the occult, sex and life after death. They are good with math and when offended can wield words like a lethal weapon. Mercury in this placement can create obsessions, mental obsessions with death and dying or preoccupation and obsession with sexual matters. In some way, at some point in life, an experience with death or the loss of a loved one, or a disturbing sexual encounter, may completely change the way these Virgos live and think. Frequent short trips and communication may be necessary to resolve a mutual financial endeavor. It could be to help a parent obtain Social Security benefits or the mate's benefits, or merely to settle an insurance matter in connection with a car accident. With this placement of Mercury, the natives are more likely to outlive their siblings.

Mercury, Ruler of the Ascendant, in the Third House in Sagittarius: As Mercury is a mutable, changeable planet, its placement in a mutable house and sign requires these Virgos to exercise strong strength of character to finish projects and to avoid scattering their forces. They are impulsive, independent and freedom loving. They are also very generous individuals who will do anything for anyone and very often promise more than what they can actually deliver because they truly want to be of service to mankind and find it difficult to say "no" to requests made of them. The Virgo Ascendant wants to be prompt for appointments, but the Sagittarius Mercury often thinks it has more time than it does, so on occasion these individuals are certain to be late and more than likely for their own funerals. They are honest people who prefer to tell the truth and say exactly what comes into their minds without pausing to consider the consequences of what they are saying; they are surprised when they discover they have hurt someone's feelings. Active physically and mentally, they are also quite changeable, bore easily and require constant stimulation to keep their attention. They may teach religion, keep books or act as secretary of a religious organization. Many travel for educational pursuits, to attend lectures or seminars, or to visit siblings who live in distant cities. They may go through a period of dealing with long distance phone calls and letter writing.

Mercury, Ruler of the Ascendant, in the Fourth House in Sagittarius: Compassionate, caring and generous to the needs and care of a parent or parent-in-law, they may have to share their home with one of them. Legal issues may arise over property belonging to a parent or in connection with sales or purchases thereof. Dissention or disagreements with the mate's siblings are possible over the property or estate of a parent-in-law. These natives may undergo periods of great activity in which family members who live in distant cities come to visit or many long distance telephone calls or letters are received. They may be from a family of strong religious background or have a sibling or brother- or sister-in-law in a religious order. Home ownership is a goal, especially one with a spacious yard that is not too close to neighbors.

Mercury, Ruler of the Ascendant in the Fourth House in Capricorn: Always wanting to be busy and fuss with something around the house, at the same time they can be discontented with their lot in life. They prefer to own a home that keeps them somewhat isolated from their neighbors, one with a lot of land around the house. These Virgos are reserved, aloof, standoffish, easily depressed and prone to see the dark side of situations. They have a great sense of detail and strive to do a thorough, systematic job of whatever is attempted. With soft aspects the mind is profound, steady, serious, contemplative and conscientious. The memory is good and they seldom forget, especially when others offend them or give them the impression they are being laughed at or talked about. Often collectors of things such as stamps or old coins, they generally are loners and somewhat indecisive, but industrious and hard working. They like to build things, especially out of wood, to enhance home surroundings, and are likely to inherit property from a parent or grandparent.

Mercury, Ruler of the Ascendant, in the Fifth House in Capricorn: There is the capacity to readily assimilate knowledge, which these natives have an uncanny way of transmitting to children at their own level of understanding. For this reason, they make good teachers who are patient, firm and responsive to the children's needs. They may be fond of cultural entertainment—opera, theater or visiting museums. This placement may limit the number of children because Virgos are aware of the responsibility and worry connected with rearing children. They have a creative flair, but in a practical sense such as cake decorating, flower arranging, writing children's books and hobbies that can be transformed into a business. Some suffer mental depression through rejection in love relationships. These individuals may assume responsibility for a sibling's child, such as providing day care. Romantic partners are either older, mature business people or work for the government in some capacity such as politician, police officer, city worker or teacher.

Mercury, Ruler of the Ascendant, in the Fifth House in Aquarius: This is a far better placement for Mercury as it is less depressive and more inclined toward positive thinking. The mind is keen, penetrating and ingenious, with good intuition. There is a strong interest in hobbies involving the occult, metaphysics and astrology. Should a child need a costume, these individuals have the capacity to come up with unique and original ideas on the spur of the moment. They make friends easily and enjoy large gatherings, groups of friends and interacting through the exchange of views and ideas. They are inclined toward romantic partners who are different, unique in their own style of appearance, intelligent, witty and friendly. Some work with gifted or autistic children. Children of Virgos are likely to be independent, belligerent and interested in unique and different subjects, moving to the beat of their own drummer.

Mercury, Ruler of the Ascendant, in the Sixth House in Aquarius: In order to maintain interest, these natives require an occupation that offers a variety of duties; they are mentally active and liable to nervous stress from overwork. This placement indicates an illness that affects the nerves and one which is likely to be difficult to cure, such as a nervous twitch; it can also indicate muscular dystrophy or polio. Occupations of interest are the computer field, astrologer, x-ray technician, secretary or bookkeeper for a credit union, club or association. Changes in duties or shifts can occur at a moment's notice. With hard aspects to Mercury in the sixth house and in a fixed sign, these natives may not adjust or adapt as readily as might be expected to changing situations or the introduction of new machinery or office techniques. They work well independently.

Mercury, Ruler of the Ascendant, in the Sixth House in Pisces: The mind is imaginative, impressionable and adjusts readily to changing situations. These individuals are heavily influenced by their working environment and need light colored walls and windows so they can observe the changing seasons; it is depressing to them to work in a dark, cellar-type room with no windows. These individuals require an atmosphere of peace and quiet in order to function properly in completing work-related duties. They work best alone, in solitude, and cannot tolerate commotion, unnecessary noise or loud laughter and chatter from others while trying to concentrate. These Virgos are interested in the medical field, as nurses or dieticians, or in metaphysical healing and hygiene. Some worry excessively and expand minor health problems out of proportion. When surgery is suggested, it is a good idea to get a second opinion as x-rays or examination records have been known to get mixed up. They should always carefully read prescription bottles to be sure the pharmacist filled them correctly, and to take only medication prescribed by a physician. There may be people in the place of employment who appear to have the best interests of these natives at heart, but they may not be entirely reliable or dependable. A brother or sister may require medication to control a health problem.

Mercury, Ruler of the Ascendant, in the Seventh House in Pisces: These natives are so romantic that they have preconceived ideas of what a marriage partner should be like. As youths, they read love stories or fairy tales of romance and princesses in castles. Some Virgos are disillusioned when they wake up and smell the coffee, seeing the marriage partner for all his or her faults and virtues. With hard aspects sometimes the Virgo has to play nursemaid and bottle washer to a mate who is certain he or she has every ailment in the medical books. Others in the immediate environment are likely to require the native's nursing services for an illness that is difficult to cure but is held in check with medication. Sometimes Virgos marry people who are substance abusers; much depends on the aspects to Mercury in the seventh house. Mental pursuits may involve partnerships, sometimes with a sibling. In either case, others may not carry their own weight in discharging duties, with the Virgo doing most of the work. These people should be careful what they say as statements can come back to haunt them in the form of litigation over what they consider to be insignificant trifles. Clarity of speech and ensuring that others understand what is said will always be a necessity to avoid being misinterpreted or misunderstood.

Mercury, Ruler of the Ascendant, in the Seventh House in Aries: This adds quickness of speech and action, and sometimes there is the tendency to exaggerate. This mind is keen, adaptable, full of new ideas and eager to grasp new ventures and opportunities. Anything that smacks of a challenge is intriguing to them. They have good leadership qualities and will take an active role in planning social affairs and parties, especially those involved with groups. Likely to marry those who are ambitious, independent and energetic, both mentally and physically, these natives may have frequent minor spats with brothers or sister of the marriage or business partner.

Mercury, Ruler of the Ascendant, in the Eighth House in Aries: Once these Virgos make up their minds, they have strong willpower and determination and it is difficult to sway them from their course of action. They may have to assertively take charge in connection with mutual funds and goods of the departed, and can aggressively pursue overdue insurance settlements, Social Security benefits that are being held up or disability benefits and Worker's Compensation for self and others. Sometimes there are unsettling situations that cause stress and worry in connection with a partner's financial affairs. They are likely to attend meetings, lectures or seminars concerned with the occult, metaphysics and astrology. The possible loss of a brother, sister, cousin or other close relative may result in mental anguish. The passionate nature likes to hear and talk about sex.

Mercury, Ruler of the Ascendant, in the Eighth House in Taurus: These Virgos have fixed opinions, strong likes and dislikes; these are not middle of the road individuals. Stubborn and set in their ideas, they are goal-oriented people who are determined to pursue their objectives in spite of all odds. They have charming and pleasing personalities, and are fond of the opposite sex but likely to marry for money and position rather than love. With a practical and conscientious mentality that is applied to areas where mutual funds and possessions can be used to the best advantage of these natives, they have sound ideas in financial management for others and make good bankers, investors and money managers. They may collect valuable letters or documents of noted personalities or art objects, and know the true value of things, hanging on to what they have already accumulated.

Mercury, Ruler of the Ascendant, in the Ninth House in Taurus: They can obtain money through freelance writing, teaching, travel, sales of foreign commodities or imports and exports. There are possible gifts or financial gain or loss through marriage or a business partner's relatives, especially brothers and sisters. The mind is serious and studious—slow to grasp knowledge, but once learned it is retained. They must be careful about verbal agreements or signing legal documents as both could have an averse effect on personal finances. With soft aspects, college tuition may be funded through scholarships or an employer-paid educational program.

Mercury, Ruler of the Ascendant, in the Ninth House in Gemini: This is a difficult placement for Mercury because it is a mutable planet in a mutable sign in a mutable house. It requires strength of character to control the restless, changeable nature that requires constant stimulation to hold the attention. Good talkers with perceptively quick and resourceful minds, they make good lawyers, marketing or advertising agents, salespeople, teachers, newspaper reporters, public speakers or writers of short articles. Their manual dexterity is also good for occupations such as court reporter, legal secretary and typist. These Virgos may move to a distant city away from their brothers and sisters or the siblings may be the ones to move (depending on the aspects to Mercury in the ninth house as this is also the ruler of the ascending sign). The college major may be changed in mid-stream, or they may drop out of one college, only to enroll in a different one.

Mercury, Ruler of the Ascendant, in the Tenth House in Gemini: The career must be intellectually stimulating, or else restlessness will hinder progress. This configuration requires a vast variety of duties in order to maintain interest. The active, able, penetrating, adaptable mind can be used resourcefully in business, and this is a good placement for teachers, city employees and fields where fluent speech can be effectively applied in business activities. As this is a dual sign, some Virgos are likely to hold two jobs simultaneously—a full-time job with a possible sideline. Through the place of employment, they are likely to work with, or come in contact with, bookstores, office supplies, stationery stores and the media, and could work with a brother or sister or follow the same career interest as a sibling.

Mercury, Ruler of the Ascendant, in the Tenth House in Cancer: These individuals may work with a parent or family member or enter into a relative's occupation. This position favors a smaller or one-person business, or a supervisory position, as these individuals are not happy unless they hold prominent positions in their chosen careers. Even then, it will be difficult to obtain a good position because Mercury in Cancer is prone to changes, and does not promise stability in career matters. Usually, the natives work steadily and then undergo a complete reversal in the employment picture, only to begin anew with a different company after a brief layoff. An older family member, sibling or parent may have some influence in the career choice; whether gainful or not depends on the aspects to Mercury in Cancer in the tenth house. This is a good placement for political positions, dealing with public commodities and all matters that involve the public. They can become emotionally and mentally upset when there is the threat of a layoff of cutback in personnel.

Mercury, Ruler of the Ascendant, in the Eleventh House in Cancer: The mind is inspirational, unique and inventive, and Mercury in a fixed house (Aquarius' natural house) gives a mind that is firmer, stronger, more determined and comprehensive than would be possible with a mutable sign. The mind is also inventive and intuitive, with an interest in the occult, astrology and the metaphysical. This placement increases the power of concentration, enabling Virgos to stick with the subject matter in spite of the tendency to scatter their energy and thoughts.

Travel is likely to be in connection with groups or attending lectures or conferences for the purpose of mental stimulation. There are many acquaintances, but some may be unreliable or troublesome. These individuals are likely to hold officer positions in connection with clubs and associations, love to socialize and exchange views and ideas, and prefer friends of intellectual capacity, some of whom are made in school or while traveling.

Mercury, Ruler of the Ascendant, in the Eleventh House in Leo: Capable of direct, positive thinking with an inventive flair to the imagination, these natives are born leaders who like nothing better than being in charge of clubs and organizations. Attracted to friends who like to participate in sports, golf, racquetball, chess and mind games, this placement stimulates the imagination and inspirational ideas that help to develop literary or creative ability. They are likely to make friends in prestigious positions who can help promote their aims and goals, and hopes and wishes are centered around career goals and obtaining a management position. The children of friends will play an important role in the lives of these natives, and some friends may suffer health setbacks in connection with the heart, back or eyes. This placement often indicates a substitute child, such as a step-child or grandchild of the marriage partner or rearing a sibling's child.

Mercury, Ruler of the Ascendant, in the Twelfth House in Leo: These individuals are fond of investigating the occult, astrology or metaphysical subjects. This placement intensifies the power of the imagination and, with proper direction, visualization, the ability to delve into the subconscious mind to "see" desired achievements, and the foresight to strive toward the culmination of those desires. To avoid animosity, these Virgos have to be careful with speech, correspondence and the expression of views and opinions. Others are likely to distort some of the contents or take the most frivolous meanings and expand them beyond recognition. At some point in life, disturbing unsigned letters reach the home or nasty, secretive phone calls cause the natives emotional upset. These disturbing situations can be avoided by staying on the straight and narrow path and by avoiding clandestine relationships. These individuals may discover secrets in connection with a brother or sister regarding a love relationship or event surrounding the affairs of a child. A child may undergo a temporary hospital stay for a mental disturbance or a suicide attempt, but much depends on the aspects to Mercury in the twelfth house.

Mercury, Ruler of the Ascendant, in the Twelfth House in Virgo: Because certain foods or beverages do not agree with the body and cause gastric upsets, these natives must be sure to take only medication prescribed by a physician and make note of those that cause allergic reactions. It is best not to share personal secrets with coworkers, who may disclose them to the detriment of the natives. There will be times when those the natives trust in the workplace will turn against them, creating mental anguish as a result of their deceptive tactics. If these Virgos work in hospitals, with chemicals or medication, or in a vocation where systematic and detailed procedures are a must, they must always take time to double check each and every piece of paper or information. If asked by a supervisor to pass a questionable issue, these natives should protect themselves by having the supervisor sign the order to prevent any possibility of being used as a scapegoat should anything go wrong in the future.

Libra Ascendant

Cardinal Air
Positive Ruler: Venus.

Libra is the Venus-ruled sign of the natural seventh house, which is the house of partnerships, justice and social interaction. For this reason it is natural for a Libra individual to be more concerned with close relationships than with family ties.

Character Traits

Libra represents balance, peace and harmony, yet the very sense of balance these individuals hope to achieve is the one they continue to disrupt from time to to time. There is a fine line between war and peace, and these individuals would rather use charm and finesse to obtain their objectives. However, if a gracious manner does not succeed in getting them what they want, they take off their white gloves and no one would believe the words that can come out of their mouths.

Companionship is foremost in their minds as Libras are miserable alone. They need affection, someone to dine with, talk with and help them make decisions. It is not that Libras are incapable of reaching decisions on their own, but rather they want to be sure they are making the right choices. Like a balance scale, they go up and down, back and forth, and often by the time the decision is finally reached, it has already been resolved by someone else. Once a Libra makes a final decision, it is settled and no one can change their minds.

Being a sociable sign and strongly interested in the opposite sex, they may have a psychological fear of going through life alone. Having a partner, if not in marriage, then at least someone to go out with, is important to their well-being and self-esteem.

Libras are not particularly enthusiastic about anything until they have thought through the subject. They love beautifully decorated homes, tasteful furnishings, fine clothes and jewelry.

Peace loving, amiable, affectionate, sociable and diplomatic, they believe in justice and fair play and prefer hearing both sides of an issue before coming to a conclusion. Libras are generally easygoing and rarely lose their tempers because they can usually see and understand the other person's viewpoint.

Neat and particular, they dislike hard or dirty work, but will do it if necessary, and can adapt themselves to any set of circumstances.

Their energy comes in spurts, either working hard or sitting around the house for days doing nothing. And, when they are in their active state, they want everyone else to work along with them. When in the inactive state, they want everyone around them to sit down and relax.

Their artistic talent can lead them into careers dealing with music, singing, dancing, the stage or television. Other career choices are those dealing with luxury items, cosmetics, hair styling or interior decorating. Their attractive features and figures are perfect for the fashion world as models. Their sense of justice often leads them into courts of law as attorneys, judges or court reporters. Others are excellent at public relations or as diplomats. Marriage counseling is another line of work that may interest them.

Physical Appearance

Individuals possess some Libra qualities and physical features if they have any of the following configurations in the natal chart:
- Libra rising
- Venus in the first house (noticeably stronger if conjunct the Ascendant)
- Venus within orb of the Ascendant degree
- Ruler of the first house in Libra
- Ruler of the first house conjunct or otherwise in close aspect with Venus
- Sun or Moon in Libra
- Sun or Moon in close aspect with Venus
- Libra intercepted in the first house

Libra rising individuals possess one or more of the following features:
- A cleft in the chin or dimples in the cheeks
- Features are not pronounced or overdone, but well-balanced
- Hair is low on the forehead and often curly
- Venus governs curves, and both face and body are based on harmony and balance of features

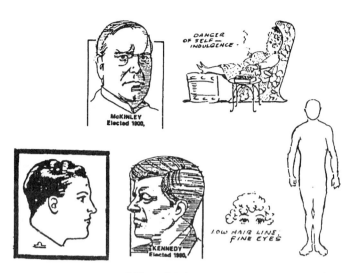

Libra Rising

- Clear skin, full lashes, full lips like a cupid's bow
- Round face with soft, fine hair; pink and white complexion becomes ruddy in middle age
- Long straight Grecian nose
- Often parts hair in the middle
- Kind expression, mouth usually well-formed, generally considered to be the most attractive and youthful looking of all the signs

Mentality

Clue Words: Impartial, just, diplomatic, considerate

The Libra mind is gentle, refined and imaginative, seeking justice and fair play with impartiality, regardless of who is involved. They possess good judgment and a well-balanced mind. Careful in their choice of words, their gentle nature would not intentionally hurt the feelings of another. The Libra mind lacks self-confidence and needs constant praise and encouragement from others. They are susceptible to the influence of companions and have little ability to change circumstances. Clever in business, they often change occupations or positions. They try to achieve their purpose through tact and diplomacy, but if that fails, they take off their white gloves and reveal a vicious temper.

Romantic Inclinations

Clue Words: Gentle, tender, affectionate, self-gratifying

Libras are affectionate and loving but desire to be repeatedly told they are attractive, sexy and wonderful or they become quite moody. They love candlelight dinners, music and a lover singing "Misty" in their ears while dancing. It's important to always give them a small token of affection, such as a stuffed animal, perfume or a single rose. They do not take the initiative for they prefer others to do the chasing. Love and companionship is important, and for this reason many of them tend to marry early in life.

Health

The general health of Libras is better than the average person. They tend to work very hard for short spurts and then just as suddenly stop and completely relax. When they work, everyone around them gets pulled into doing their share and when they relax they prefer everyone else to relax with them. With this kind of a balanced system, Libras will never overwork themselves. Other areas are the kidneys, ovaries, bladder, diabetes, skin disorders and varicose veins.

Notes on Venus

Venus always rules the feminine gender and women will touch each individual's life at some time according to the sign, house position and aspects.

Venus always governs the marriage partner. The house, sign and aspects reveal where and how these natives are likely to meet their partners, as well as some of the partner's general characteristics. Venus is the natural ruler of money and by house, sign and aspects reveals how Venus financially affects the lives of these native, how they earn income and who will help them gain or lose financially.

Venus sits quietly in the natal chart, requiring major transits or an eclipse to push it into action. If the ruler of the third, eleventh, sixth, ninth and so forth are in aspect with natal Venus, then it is likely to be a female who is going to bring activity into the native's life. Major planets or an eclipse in Gemini, Aquarius, Virgo, Sagittarius or Pisces in aspect with Venus also produces activity with women—sisters, friends, coworkers, in-laws or twelfth house secret enemies.

If the ruler of the second or eighth house makes an aspect with natal Venus, it brings gifts or financial gain or loss. Also, any major transit or an eclipse in the money house (second or eighth) or money sign of Taurus or Scorpio, and in aspect with Venus, may bring a gift or money depending on the aspects. This may occur also if transiting Venus is in the natal second or eighth house and aspecting a natal planet which in turn is in aspect with a major transit or an eclipse. Transiting Venus does not have enough power on its own and requires a major transit or an eclipse in aspect at the same time to produce an important event.

If the marriage partner is to come to the fore, the seventh house ruler, by transit, will aspect Venus, transits in the seventh will aspect natal Venus or major planets, an eclipse in Libra will aspect natal Venus or transiting Venus will be in the seventh house in aspect with major transits or eclipses.

Ascendant Ruler in Signs and Houses

Venus, Ruler of the Ascendant, in the First House in Libra: This placement usually gives greater beauty and elegance and natural good looks. Because of the triple connotation of Libra rising and Venus in Libra, one has to give serious judgment to the aspects Venus receives from other planets. With no hard aspects, these individuals make excellent marriage or school counselors. Women are especially attractive, with a Grecian profile. Some are certain to be interested in modeling, acting, singing or working in some way with things of beauty. Hair styling, dress designing, interior decorating and public relations are a few vocational interests. Men are also quite good looking, with softer appearances. Kirk Douglas is a typical example as he has a deep cleft in his chin, and is masculine yet at the same time has a certain charm and sex appeal that softens his appearance. These men often wear well-made suits and clothing, and gold chains around their necks and expensive rings on their fingers. If they don't enter the creative arts, they usually enter fields where sound judgment is required: police officer, judge, attorney, court reporter, diplomat. Those with less education may work for the banking industry as mortgage advisors, bookkeepers or receptionists or in public relations. Men with this placement generally get along very well with women unless there are hard aspects to Venus. These men possess a certain charm that women just can't resist. Some are excellent dancers and the type who sing "Misty" in a lover's ear. And, they always remember to bring a small gift, a rose or just a stuffed animal. They are thoughtful individuals who seldom forget birthdays or special occasions. Women usually have sing-song voices, and always seem to use the greeting "Hello, darling, how are you today?" They seldom chase men as they feel it is the man's role to do the chasing. Either sex can be gracious to the extreme, yet when the occasion calls for it, they can stand up and fight for what they believe is right. This is why so many military men are born under the sign of Libra; Dwight D. Eisenhower and John F. Kennedy are typical examples.

Venus, Ruler of the Ascendant, in the First House in Scorpio: A great deal depends on the aspects involving Venus in Scorpio. I have a client with soft aspects to her ruler Venus in Scorpio in her first house and she is a caring, sympathetic person who is always raising funds for one cause or another. I have a male client with Libra rising and Venus in his first house in Scorpio square natal Saturn in his fourth house in Aquarius. He is a demanding dictator who expects his children and wife to conform to his wishes. A jealous, cynical, possessive individual who goes into rages of temper and violence, at social occasions outside the home everyone tells his wife how lucky she is to be married to him. His Libra charm always sways those outside his immediate environment. He is a bank manager who is well-known in his city, and his wife was having an affair with a priest (he has Jupiter in his twelfth house in Libra). When he arrived home early one day and found a priest's collar on his dresser, he went into a violent rage. His wife became so terrified of him that she tried to commit suicide and, as a result, he talked his physician friend into admitting her to a mental hospital and signed for shock treatments which she did not need. That was the Venus in Scorpio (revenge) square Saturn in the fourth house (family member) in the sign of shock treatments (Aquarius). Either sex is possessive and resents social injustice, and there can be romantic problems with an unconscious desire for a love affair and social events. With normal self-control, emotional pitfalls can be avoided.

Venus, Ruler of the Ascendant, in the Second House in Scorpio: As this is the house of personal finances, there may be a chance of monetary gain through the partner, an inheritance, an insurance settlement and other mutual funds. If Venus receives soft aspects, there can be substantial luck or financial gain in relation to income or business. A female will play an important role in connection with personal finances. Libra rising individuals with this placement may earn income through the medical field, as insurance adjuster or agents, working in a payroll department or selling undergarments. There is the possibility of contact with the Internal Revenue Service, so they should keep good income tax records in case of an audit.

Venus, Ruler of the Ascendant, in the Second House in Sagittarius: Luck and finances go hand-in-hand with this placement. Just when the natives are down to their last dollar, something always arrives in the nick of time. This placement generally brings money from distant places through published material, teaching, lecturing or contacts with people living in distant cities. Long distance telephone operators would have such placement, as would those who deal with matters connected with beauty equipment or cosmetics. Some may drive interstate trucks or other large equipment as part of their job duties. These natives have well-balanced minds that are full of ideas, and need to develop strength of character for they tend to scatter their energy into too many projects.

Venus, Ruler of the Ascendant, in the Third House in Sagittarius: These individuals are generous, kind, amiable and respected for their justice and integrity. However, they can carry their honesty to the extreme and blurt out statements without proper forethought, and then be devastated when they discover they have hurt another person's feelings. A sister is likely to move to a distant city or these natives move away from their immediate families. As a result, there is likely to be much letter writing and long distance phone calls connected with third house matters. If natal Jupiter or the condition of the ninth house verify, there is a possibility they may teach religious classes or be teachers in religious schools. There are contacts with influential people and with those of a different background, race or culture. This is a good placement for creative writers. They prefer to travel with a companion. Some individuals with this placement are long distance telephone operators or work in the mail room of a company that receives letters from a distance or through foreign countries. Sometimes they travel to visit brothers- and sisters-in-law who live in faraway cities. If Venus has hard aspects natally or receives hard aspects from major transits or an eclipse, the natives could become involved in sticky lawsuits with neighbors.

Venus, Ruler of the Ascendant, in the Third House in Capricorn: Despite the desire for companionship, there is a degree of reserve and some difficulty at times in the expression of feelings. It is important for these individuals to permit others to express their feelings first; then personal responses will be less difficult, for unless a lead is given, there will be a sense of restriction and inhibition which will not be easy to overcome. These individuals have great mental sensitivity and any rebuff as a result of making personal mistakes will intensify the feeling of emotional hurt and can cause a sense of humiliation. This may weaken the character and permit mental depression to take hold. Sometimes this aspect indicates a loner, one who only permits a select few into the social circle. Generally, they have companions that they keep intact from early school years. As this is the third house of communication, these natives are reserved in their speech and careful about what they say. Should Venus receive hard aspects, they can be abrupt in their manner of speaking and utter cutting remarks on occasion. These natives can be only children or have responsibility for a sibling while parents work.

Venus, Ruler of the Ascendant, in the Fourth House in Capricorn: As the fourth house governs emotional responses, these individuals are even more sensitive in the expression of their emotional feelings. They seldom make advances in relationships, for they fear rejection and ridicule. This placement can give good business sense with real estate or property matters. They are likely to meet someone of the opposite sex at some time in life, and be baffled concerning the relationship, finding it quite difficult to determine whether the object of their affection has any emotional feelings toward them. They don't want to let go of the relationship, yet at the same time feel it is going nowhere. There is the possibility of caring for or having responsibility for a parent. When it comes to home surroundings, they prefer one that is not too close to neighbors as they want a certain degree of privacy. Some like a lot of land surrounding their property, not necessarily wooded. In a man's chart, there is a strong possibility that he may one day share a living arrangement with an older woman or one of Capricorn coloring.

Venus, Ruler of the Ascendant, in the Fourth House in Aquarius: These individuals are unique with an independent streak and intensity of emotional expression. There may be an interest in unusual subject matter, such as astrology, the occult and other scientific matters. The home rarely runs on an even keel as there are unexpected events that may disrupt the daily routine. Sometimes the home is a social gathering place for friends or a meeting place for clubs and organizations. There is the possibility of sudden gains or losses through property or finances through the partner, parents or close family members. In a man's chart, an interesting relationship may be formed with an older woman. It is not unusual in some cases that a Libra may share living quarters with a girlfriend. The unexpected is likely to happen while entertaining in the home. There may be unexpected loss or separation through one of the parents. These natives should avoid unconventional behavior, emotional restlessness or unusual experiences, for once the bars are down it will be difficult to build them up again. If Venus is in the fourth house but in the sign that governs the fifth house, there may be one particular child who will be different from the norm, or suffer an incurable illness.

Venus, Ruler of the Ascendant, in the Fifth House in Aquarius: Creative inventiveness with a good head for business could turn a hobby into a spare time money making project. The study of astrology or the occult could be very productive for future financial gains. These individuals are generally attractive, interesting, magnetic and fascinating. They have the ability to talk on many subjects as if they were well-versed in them. They have their own unique style of dress and seldom follow the latest fashion trend. This could be an exciting placement for social affairs and romance, but they may be inclined toward the unconventional in relationships. Women with this placement may experience difficulty in childbirth. Depending on the aspects, they could have borderline geniuses for children or those who need special tutoring and personal attention.

Venus, Ruler of the Ascendant, in the Fifth House in Pisces: These individuals do not always see their romantic partners as they really are. This tendency toward idealism can cause problems in personal and romantic relationships. They have to be especially careful of becoming entangled with romantic interests who have peculiar emotional or sexual ideas. Involvement with people of questionable character could harm their reputation. The objects of their affections may be already married, secret drinkers or drug abusers. Self-deception and the emotions can lead them astray, and they should guard against being taken in or misguided by their feelings. Not all is negative with Venus in Pisces in the fifth house, as they can meet musicians, artists, police officers, physicians or sensitive people who also have been hurt by deceptive partners. This is an excellent placement for those who enjoy family outings, picnics and small intimate social gatherings. These individuals could have a creative flair in the arts, music or imaginative writing. They may have children who are sensitive. Venus does not always indicate a female child; instead, a male child may at first prove to be a disappointment because he avoids participation in sports and leans more toward art. Should Venus in Pisces be in the fifth house but on the cusp of the sixth house, women may develop unusual health problems during pregnancy.

Venus, Ruler of the Ascendant, in the Sixth House in Pisces: Whatever arouses the feelings of these natives depends on the state of their emotions for they are easily affected by surrounding conditions. Therefore, it is imperative that they always maintain a well-balanced and harmonious atmosphere at their place of employment. These individuals require a quiet place for discharging work-related duties. Chaotic conditions, unnecessary noise and confusion make it extremely difficult for them to concentrate. There may be opportunities for a clandestine affair with someone through contacts at work, but this temptation should be avoided at all costs for it will make matters uncomfortable in the workplace. These natives should never confide secrets to coworkers because they are likely to backfire. Whenever surgery is advised by a physician, the possibility of error exists; it is best to seek a second opinion. If these people work with chemicals, gasses or oils, they should be careful in handling them as they may be sensitive to the products. When doing housework, they should never attempt to clean their own ovens in a closed room or even consider mixing different types of cleaning substances as they could be overcome by the fumes.

Venus, Ruler of the Ascendant, in the Sixth House in Aries: This is an excellent placement for a man's chart as it adds a strong touch of masculinity to Libra rising. These natives are more aggressive, independent and assertive in discharging their work-related duties, and are more apt to take charge in times of crisis or when difficulties arise through coworkers or as a result of working conditions. They are not happy in subordinate roles as they do not tolerate being bossed. This is a difficult configuration for women as they will tend to be in competition with men at work, and prefer the role of boss or supervisor. An "I'll do it myself" attitude can rub men the wrong way. Because the ruling planet is in Aries in the sixth house, women are more likely to become romantically involved on an impulse with someone who works for them, is a coworker or is encountered through work-related contacts. If marriage results between a boss and an employee, friction can result later when the man has to take orders from his wife. Health concerns can be migraine headaches, sinus conditions, a scar on the head or face through an accident at work, a sudden flareup of fever or kidney problems due to inadequate consumption of water on a daily basis.

Venus, Ruler of the Ascendant, in the Seventh House in Aries: Demonstrative and generous with affections, warm-hearted and attracted to those of the opposite sex, marriage and partnerships play an important part for these natives in producing personal happiness and material benefits. Popularity with the general public helps in the achievement of success, and artistic or creative ability is usually above average. In a woman's chart, this is a rather difficult placement because Venus is not in the best of signs. These females seek a marriage or business partner who is ambitious, aggressive, independent and decisive. If they marry someone who does not fit that bill, and is something of a wimp, they soon lose respect for the mate and divorce may be the end result. They are seeking partners for whom they do not have to make decisions and relationships in which they are not forced to take the lead in every situation. A man who says "Honey, whatever you say is fine with me" won't go over big with these Libra women. They're looking for a "man's man," one who knows what he wants and how to obtain it, a decisive individual who is well-liked and respected by others because of his integrity and ability to achieve a high position in life. If this placement of Venus in Aries in the seventh house occurs in a man's chart, the situation is a bit different. Men with this placement are looking for women who can wear the "pants" in the family, who can make decisions on their own without having to constantly inquire, "Honey, what do you think I should do about this situation?"

Venus, Ruler of the Ascendant, in the Seventh House in Taurus: This placement adds a great deal of personal magnetism to the personality, which ensures the good will and assistance of others. These natives are amiable, diplomatic, neat and particular, but they dislike hard or dirty work while retaining the capacity to work hard if necessary. They love peace and harmony and are averse to dissention and cruelty. Because Taurus is probably on the cusp of the eighth house, they seek marriage or business partners who can enhance financial security, people who either have money or have the ways and means to obtain it. Depending on the aspects, money is gained or lost through the resources of others, marriage or business partners, or close associates.

Venus, Ruler of the Ascendant, in the Eighth House in Taurus: Marriage, partnerships, insurance, inheritance and investments are likely to be vital issues, producing either great benefits or heavy losses. The position of Venus in the eighth house can assist with charm and finesse in smoothing out any difficulties concerning such things as insurance claims, taxation, wills, legacies, probate problems and other affairs governed by mutual funds. The love nature is extreme and these natives may marry for money. Often there are two marriages; the first may occur early in life but the second is likely to be the happiest. In either sex, this placement of Venus in the eighth house endows a strong sexual appearance. They often dress seductively or the facial expressions are sensual.

Venus, Ruler of the Ascendant, in the Eighth House in Gemini: These individuals can be very aloof and dislike being touched or caressed. When sexual affection is expressed it is more of the mind than the body. This placement can accentuate certain secret emotional or even passionate desires that are kept on the mental plane, and there is the likelihood of more than one marriage due to the duality of Gemini. This placement increases the prospects of gain through inheritance, legacies, insurance settlements, wills or joint financial matters. The individuals usually receive gifts, which can take the form of money, possessions or property, through others who are well-disposed toward them. Venus in Gemini (documents) in the eighth house (mutual finances) is more likely to sign prenuptial agreements. Jackie Kennedy Onassis had this placement, and both times she married for money; the second one demanded a prenuptial contract. As the eighth house represents surgery, these natives may have an operation on the throat or kidneys.

Venus, Ruler of the Ascendant, in the Ninth House in Gemini: This is an excellent placement for Venus as it makes the natives kind, helpful, gentle with a cultured intellect and appreciative of every form of mental improvement. They have good taste in artistic matters, an intense love of beauty, great generosity and a sympathetic understanding of others. There may be a sibling who lives in a distant city, or these natives move away from their early environment. If there are indications that the native will move away from the place of birth, weigh carefully the fourth house, planets therein and the rulers thereof. Then weigh the third house of brothers and sisters, planets therein and rulers thereof for possible indications that it will be a sibling who will relocate. Venus in the ninth house likes to have a companion while traveling and prefers personal comfort to roughing it. Marriage is possible to someone of a different background—social or educational level, religion, race or with a foreign accent. More than one marriage is likely due to the dualistic nature of Gemini; however, check the condition of the seventh house for verification. As this is the third house of the seventh house partner, there may be a sister- or brother-in-law with Taurus or Libra coloring (that is, Taurus or Libra rising, Moon or Sun in Taurus or Libra, Venus in the first house, Venus in aspect with the Ascendant or the ruler of the Ascendant in Taurus or Libra). The general effect of religion may come through the feminine side and it is possible if Jupiter, a natal planet is Sagittarius or the twelfth house confirm these findings.

Venus, Ruler of the Ascendant, in the Ninth House in Cancer: Exceptionally emotional with a somewhat clinging love nature, these natives are very sensitive with deep, quiet feelings. Although they are intensely sentimental and have strong family ties, they love to travel but are always happy to return to the nest. There may be a strong interest in the study of astrology, metaphysics or the occult. As this is a mutable house, there is the possibility of several love affairs with those of different backgrounds or social levels, or secret unconventional attractions, quite possibly with someone of a vastly different age, either much older or younger. There is a good chance of property gain through in-laws or through a parent who may reside in a distant city. There may be a desire to own a country cottage for quiet getaway weekends. Hard aspects could indicate obstacles with marriage plans, where the parents or future parents-in-law do not approve of the union, or there may be financial, health or occupational difficulties.

Venus, ruler of the Ascendant, in the Tenth House in Cancer: This is not the best placement for Venus in Cancer for neither Venus nor Cancer are compatible with the tenth, Capricorn's natural house. It tends to reserve the emotions and the affectionate nature. The native is ultra-sensitive and does not take criticism or rejection lightly. This inhibited emotional factor often interferes with the marriage state and sometimes divorce is the result. The nature is ambitious, diplomatic, favors popularity, endows a pleasant manner and is protective of the reputation. This type of personality endears the natives to their bosses and those in authority who view the native as conscientious and courteous with the makings of a good company public relations person. Success is likely to be accelerated as a result of the benevolent interest of superiors, and sometimes the natives may combine social functions and career matters. This is good for financial professions such as banking, accounting, insurance and real estate, as well as commercial art, hair styling, interior decorating, payroll or money that deals with the general public such as the lottery (Venus in the public sign of Cancer).

Venus, Ruler of the Ascendant, in the Tenth House in Leo: Leo blends well with the Libra ascending sign. It adds a regal, upright bearing to the figure and the women usually have their hair parted in the middle with bangs on the forehead. They are good looking with a cleft in the chin or dimples in their cheeks. Even men with slightly thinning hair are a handsome lot. These individuals have to be the best in their chosen career and do well in the entertainment or public relations field where they are in the public eye. It is difficult for these individuals to sit behind a desk doing routine, boring tasks. At some time in life, they will have to blend social, public or artistic matters with ordinary business or professional activities. For example, the boss may request help in entertaining out-of-town bigwigs at a dinner or social gathering. Due to Leo, a position of management or supervision is highly marked for career interest, as well as professions connected with children, sports, finances, hair styling, acting, fashion, decorating or the lottery.

Venus, Ruler of the Ascendant, in the Eleventh House in Leo: This placement of Venus adds a touch of glamour and magnetic and dynamic qualities to the character. The tenth house has the coloring of Saturn and tends to subdue the qualities of Venus in emotional expression. These individuals, at some point in life, hold responsible positions with clubs or organizations or serve as officers. Social planners fall under this combination, and the natives may join groups such as Parents Without Partners due to the Leo (children) connection. Either sex may be drawn toward groups that deal with sports—golf, tennis, bowling, racquetball—especially if they get together socially after each game. Because Venus is the natural ruler of the marriage partner, it is possible for these natives to have step-children as the eleventh house is the fifth house of the seventh house. It is also possible they will meet their future mates at a group activity. Care is necessary with this placement as Leo is the natural ruler of romance; sometimes a casual friendship can turn into a romantic affair which can be difficult if one or the other is married.

Venus, Ruler of the Ascendant in the Eleventh House in Virgo: This placement of Venus in Virgo is not as attractive as Leo, however there is the tendency to dress well, selecting clothing of good taste. There is likely to be a small hump on the nose and thinning hair as the individual matures, but the body is well-formed, being somewhat tall and slim. There is more selectivity in choosing friends and acquaintances. The eleventh house is group-related creativity, and Venus in Virgo in the eleventh house produces creativity on a practical level. Emphasis is placed on intellectual rather than social interaction. Even when engaging in social activities there is certain to be an atmosphere of learning or a practical exchange of ideas. Sometimes friends are formed through the workplace, and job opportunities can result through suggestions made by close friends. Depending on the aspects to Venus, some may have to attend conventions or seminars in connection with their occupation. They may come in contact with acquaintances who will drive them to utter despair and create nervous stomach upsets with their constant complaining about health problems. These natives must be careful not to be too critical and faulting of close ties for it is impossible for them to share the same degree of perfection. Bonds of affection are likely to be formed with someone whose vocation is similar. This placement often draws the natives toward unusual occupations such as astrology, spiritual healing, metaphysics, weather forecasting, computers, x-ray equipment and electronics.

Venus, Ruler of the Ascendant in the Twelfth House in Virgo: These individuals may not be as attractive as other sign placements, but are endowed with well-proportioned bodies. Sometimes there is a hump on the bridge of the nose and the hair may thin out later in life. The house cusp with Virgo indicates the type of work the natives may be interested in or the people they may work with at some point in life. Venus in Virgo in the twelfth house is excellent for working in places of isolation—hospitals, institutions, prisons. There is more stress placed on the desire for companionship and a willingness to please can cause these people to form attachments that may require giving up personal freedom or making necessary sacrifices for others in exchange for their affection. With hard aspects, deception may come through association with co-workers. These natives are more likely to be sensitive to certain drugs or medication and foods. It may be necessary to play "second banana" in the occupation, and secluded occupations are likely to offer the maximum possibilities of gain.

Venus, Ruler of the Ascendant, in the Twelfth House in Libra: These natives are exquisite looking with soft, dreamy eyes and a creamy complexion. They can be easily swayed through their emotions and through sympathy, and are likely to find greater satisfaction with secluded occupations that keep them behind the scenes in quiet privacy.

There is a peaceful undercurrent to their emotions which permits them to be happy in a life that most others would consider lonely. The emotions are extremely vulnerable and temperamental, and they can open themselves to heart-rending hurts if they yield to anything that smacks of a clandestine affair (because of the Libra connotation, one or both are certain to be married). This is not an easy situation for the twelfth house also governs secret sorrows; sometimes they may have to break off an attachment in order to protect the marital partner, who may suffer through these acts of indiscretion. Women can become secret enemies and it is not always easy to detect who they are while they are conniving against others. This is an excellent placement for psychic and metaphysical research, chemistry, medicine and the creative arts, and these natives can achieve pleasure and success through working with large animals, especially horses. They can benefit through volunteer work or charitable institutions, and many with this configuration work in hospitals or with photography, or operate dance studios or tech art or music. Either sex can work well with law enforcement, counseling or psychology.

Scorpio Ascendant

Fixed Water
Negative Ruler: Pluto

Scorpio is the Pluto-ruled sign of the natural eighth house and represents life after death, passion, sexuality and deep intensity of emotions. It is for this reason that so many Scorpio natives enter the study of metaphysics, Karma and reincarnation.

Character Traits

The Scorpio nature is one of strong determination, willpower and fixity of purpose. Their energy is unsurpassed, giving them the capacity to work long and hard, achieving efforts of unlimited capacity.

Strongly loyal, they expect the same in return whether from employees, friends or family members. They possess an explosive temper and in some cases a somewhat vindictive streak, seldom forgetting a person who has slighted them in some way. They will get even, if it takes ten years.

Whether the Scorpio person is aware of it or not, many of them possess natural psychic ability, while others probe into the deep mysteries of life in the hereafter. Death becomes either an obsession or is accepted in terms of its true meaning—rebirth—for only through death can man rise and be born again.

Scorpio represents power and likes to change and move things and see how they work; they are born investigators and researchers.

Scorpios are seldom content and continue to tear themselves apart, trying hard to seek perfection in some particular capacity.

There are two distinct types: those that sting and those that don't. The first one is the lower type, vindictive know-it-alls who will never admit they are wrong. Outwardly they give the impression of a fine character, but they can be sarcastic with a mean disposition. They cannot be trusted because they are only interested in promoting personal gain. Some are frequently over-sexed.

The higher plane is courageous, loyal and dynamic. They have a personality that commands respect and their executive ability is tremendous. While they are not lovers of hard work, they will work hard if necessary to achieve success.

Both types have strong likes and dislikes and may be lacking in tact and finesse. They are strong, forceful, energetic individuals capable of immense feats of endurance and courage.

Very ambitious, they seldom admit defeat and are somewhat indiscreet and given to excess. They can be sarcastic and ride roughshod over others, but resent being treated in a similar fashion.

Self-confident and reserved, they carry themselves with an air of dignity and can be willful, impulsive and daring when put to the test. They have fixed views and are goal oriented. There may be inner conflicts that continually push them to strive for perfection, and they often connect with group action of various kinds.

Pluto in the horoscope shows what direction the dictates of the subconscious mind may be urging individuals to take. These urges can be quite powerful and all the more difficult to deal with because individuals may not be aware of the real reason for their urges to act in a certain way.

Many have a gift or love of healing and make excellent doctors, nurses, dentists and surgeons. Research is second nature along with engineering, mechanics, metaphysics, astrology or the occult. Some work with payroll, mortgages, insurance, wills or scheduling of time sheets.

Physical Appearance

Individuals possess some Scorpio qualities and physical features if they have any of the following configurations in the natal chart:
- Scorpio rising
- Pluto in the first house (noticeably strong if conjunct the Ascendant
- Pluto within orb of aspect with the Ascendant
- Ruler of the first house cusp in Scorpio
- Ruler of the first house cusp conjunct or otherwise in close aspect with Pluto
- Sun or Moon in Scorpio
- Sun or Moon in close aspect with Pluto
- Scorpio intercepted in the first house

Scorpio rising individuals possess one or more of the following

  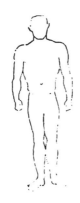

Joan Crawford

Scorpio Rising

Joan Crawford has Scorpio rising with the ruler, Pluto, in the eighth house in Gemini. Note her piercing eyes and arched, pointed eyebrows typical of many Scorpio rising individuals.

features:
- Usually of average height and a robust constitution
- Strong physique with an inclination to stoutness
- Nose is the most prominent feature, sometimes being large with a hump; a high hump indicates aggressiveness and a low hump indicates defensiveness
- Dark, sharp, piercing eyes
- Broad, square face with strong marked angles
- Often has heavy eyebrows which meet at the bridge of the nose, and sometimes come to a sharp point on top
- Dusky complexion, and dark, bushy hair that may have a reddish glint when the sun shines on it
- Short, thick neck that is similar to Taurus
- Large teeth, and sometimes there is a space between the upper front teeth
- Women are usually shapely, active and hip-swingers
- Women often wear their hair low on the forehead and close to the eyes at the side of the temples in a sort of pixy style

Mentality

Clue words: Penetrating, fixed, calculating, forceful, secretive, suspicious

The Scorpio person is shrewd, with deep powers of concentration and observation and a penetrating mind with the capacity for deductive qualities that enables them to read the character of others. Abruptness in speech is common for their tempers are short. They can be sarcastic, and secretive regarding personal and financial affairs. Excellent researchers and investigators, they can dig into the core of any problem. Sometimes perfectionists to a fault, they may demand the same kind of perfection from those in their immediate environment.

Romantic Inclinations

Clue Words: Possessive, passionate, jealous, demanding, protective

The Scorpio sex drive is extremely strong, possessive and tinged with jealousy. Despite the intensity of their sexual nature, they have strong willpower and can exercise self-control when the occasion calls for it. If Scorpios are to function properly in everyday affairs, they must have periodic sexual release; otherwise they become frustrated and ill-tempered. Extremely loyal and expecting the same in return, they are possessive, domineering and jealous in any love relationship. They can become vindictive if unfairly rejected.

Health

Scorpios can overwork to the point where they go for long periods on short hours of rest, and then when they become ill from exhaustion they are very, very ill.

Scorpio rules the urinary and regenerative organs, nose, anus, bladder, appendix and pelvis. Ailments are: piles, ruptures, fistulas, venereal disease, infectious diseases, ailments arising from excess and heart, throat and blood disorders.

Notes on Pluto

Pluto is a difficult planet to comprehend. What it does is to force people to dig deep into themselves and understand their deeper motivations. In the psychological sense, Pluto represents the subconscious mind of the individual and, in the horoscope, shows the direction the dictates of the subconscious mind may be urging the individual to act. These urges can be very powerful and all the more difficult to deal with because individuals may not be aware of the real reason their urges act in a certain way.

Whatever sign Pluto is in will intensify the motivational influence of that sign. Pluto also will intensify the energy of the planet it is in close aspect with according to the sign and house position.

Ascendant Ruler in Signs and Houses

Pluto, Ruler of the Ascendant, in the First House in Scorpio: The only generation to feel the effects of its ruling planet in Scorpio are those born between November 5, 1983 and November 10, 1995. Much depends upon the aspects to natal Pluto, but in a general sense, these individuals will have a strong, forceful, energetic nature, capable of immense feats of endurance and courage. Seldom will they admit defeat. They may experience impulsive love affairs, and the mind is active with dynamic energy. Not everyone with this configuration will have the same intensity for research and investigative projects; give serious consideration to the eighth house (natural house of Scorpio and Pluto) and weigh the ruler of the natal eighth house and planets therein for the direction in which these individuals will pursue strong, self-centered interests. These individuals are likely to have a "law unto themselves" personality. They will quietly listen to unsolicited advice and then do what they had planned to do in the first place. As they mature, mutual funds, death, insurance or an inheritance will play an important role in their lives through professional and personal experiences. They can have a cutting or sarcastic manner of speech and in some cases are vindictive, depending on the aspects that Pluto receives. Their sharp, cool and collected mentality makes a good police officer, military person, surgeon, nurse, paramedic, detective, trouble shooter, Internal Revenue Service auditor or income tax adjustor. Pluto can cause many upheavals and turning points in life and how these individuals react to them can make or break them. This placement of Pluto in Scorpio does intensify the characteristics of the rising sign, and these individuals may try to attain success in life through brutal and ruthless means. This can lead to obsessional tendencies, dictatorship or rule by force. They may experience violent disputes, quarrels, injuries or accidents, or require surgery.

Pluto, Ruler of the Ascendant, in the First House in Sagittarius: It takes several hundred years for Pluto to travel through all twelve signs of the zodiac. It entered Sagittarius on January 17, 1995 and will leave the sign on November 26, 2008. The general outlook on life is expanded and there is a capacity for enthusiasm and enjoyment of life. Leadership qualities are a marked influence. There is also an acute awareness of the need to create desirable social conditions. Travel, education and religion are pronounced, and this could be the mark of the perpetual student, always seeking new and different things to learn. Sometimes relocation is necessary as the natives may feel they are in stagnant conditions and need new directions that may be found in different locations. There is a striving for attainment of power and authority, and they can be aggressive and impulsive, which may not be evident to observers because they use secretive and physical means of accomplishing their purpose. With favorable aspects, they best express themselves through occupations dealing with courts of law, including judge, attorney, court reporter or bailiff. Others may want to write or work for the local newspaper. With proper direction and education, the intensity of the Scorpio Ascendant can best be expressed through writing, teaching or working for the publishing and printing industry.

Pluto, Ruler of the Ascendant, in Sagittarius in the Second House: Sagittarius is adaptable and enables the native to accept change and come to terms with new phases in life with little difficulty, especially those that affect personal finances. There is a desire to attain financial success through writing, travel, publication, religion or teaching. They may experience unusual contacts or acquaintances that will require a readjustment of conditions or circumstances connected with personal funds or possessions, quite possibly involving in-laws, foreigners, courts of law or people living in distant places. This placement can offer excellent financial protection, and can produce financial gains when needed; for example, a bill arrives when the native is short of funds and then out of the blue a refund check or other monetary resource arrives in the nick of time. These individuals can expect periodic changes in financial standing, and possible gain or loss through lawsuits, inheritance through in-laws, and insurance settlements or published material. They should not risk possessions or financial endeavors on a hunch or through gambling. How Pluto in Sagittarius will operate is determined by the condition of the ninth house ruler, parents therein and the house, sign and aspects to natal Jupiter.

Pluto, Ruler of the Ascendant, in Capricorn in the Second House: This is a sign that individuals of the current generation have not yet experienced. Pluto enters Capricorn on January 26, 2008 and leaves on November 18, 2024. Capricorn is not the best sign position for Pluto, for it indicates that the natives will have to work hard with heavy laborious efforts in the accumulation of personal income. Depending on the aspects, they may gain or lose possessions or finances through an inheritance, government affairs or an authoritative figure. This placement tends to harden the outlook on life, coloring it with a serious and grumbling disposition. Often it is the mark of a loner. Replacement of the knee or other joints may be required. This is a good placement for those who earn their income by working for the government, the lottery, unemployment bureau, Worker's Compensation, Internal Revenue Service or the welfare department, to name a few. There may be a struggle to overcome the indifference and even the bad influence of others who may go out of their way to make life and earning potential difficult for the native.

Pluto, Ruler of the Ascendant, in Capricorn in the Third House: There is a need for self-expression as well as respect of others. The natives may work with heavy duty trucks, excavation or tunneling or in occupations that deal with death certificates, government payroll or scheduling of employee time sheets. They develop a cynical, suspicious and non-communicative tendency, and may go out of their way to seek solitude. Incorrect learning habits developed over the years may have to be psychologically eradicated, and they can be mentally sensitive, easily offended and have a tendency to shut themselves off from their immediate environment. Some have an abrupt, cold, detached or brutal way of speaking with others that can be rather irritating. These individuals may work for the government or large corporations where responsibility for secret information pertaining to matters of importance is a must. What these people think and how they communicate is likely to have serious consequences on success or failure in life. Death of parents early in life may create a responsible position in the care and rearing of brothers and sisters. To determine how the Scorpio rising individual will utilize Pluto in Capricorn in the third, weigh the ruler of the tenth house, planets therein and the house, sign and aspects to natal Saturn, ruler of Pluto's sign position.

Pluto, Ruler of the Ascendant, in Aquarius in the Third House: This is also a sign the current generation has not experienced. Pluto enters Aquarius on March 23, 2023 and leaves on January 18, 2044. There is great compulsion for seeking personal independence and freedom in mental pursuits of unusual studies: astrology, metaphysics, the occult, science, computers, technology, engineering and weather forecasting are a few of the possible lines of interest. However, certain subject matter can turn into obsessive research and study to the point of ignoring those in the immediate surroundings. These individuals do not tolerate being bossed and require a lot of elbow room. There is resistance to dictatorial attitudes and they should guard against the tendency for determination to deteriorate into obstinacy. Mental powers for inventive ideas are strong, and the sense of humor may be way out or weird and cutting or sarcastic at times. They need to be involved with groups that are on the same mental plane. These natives may be separated abruptly from brothers or sisters due to a catastrophe such as an airplane crash, tornado, earthquake or other natural disaster. A sibling could be a borderline genius or mentally retarded. Check the condition of the eleventh house, the ruler of the house cusp, planets therein and the house, sign and aspects to natal Uranus, ruler of Pluto's sign position.

Pluto, Ruler of the Ascendant, in the Fourth House in Aquarius: These individuals will resist any kind of family interference, as the Pluto compulsiveness will operate within the home environment and the emotional depths of the psychological life. There is a need to be in control of the domestic sphere and family affairs. If they do not approve of the situation in the immediate home environment, everyone in the family must suffer as they attempt to change it. Tension seems to build up until a sudden explosive point has been reached; then everyone in the family runs for cover. They are non-conformist with a need for excitement; an uneventful home life has little appeal. This can indicate a home life which is subject to all sorts of upheavals and battles due to wilfulness and obstinacy. The home structure may need to be rebuilt or the natives may be placed in the sudden and unexpected position of having to begin anew due to a major catastrophe that has altered the course of life. This could range from sudden loss of a parent or unexpected national disasters that destroy the home.

Pluto, Ruler of the Ascendant, in the Fourth House in Pisces: Pluto in Pisces is another placement the present generation has not yet experienced. It enters Pisces on March 9, 2043 and leaves the sign on February 22, 2068. With this placement, there is utilization of psychic forces, and a strong urge for security, a home or a place where the natives can retreat to escape periodically from the negative influences of the outside world. These individuals are able to control exactly what goes on in the environment through the use of unusual personal influence. A reorientation may be necessary in connection with one's deepest feelings, inner peace and contentment in order to obtain a steadfast sense of security. This placement sometimes introduces step-parents or foster parents as a result of unforeseen circumstances—the necessity to be reared by someone other than the biological parents. With hard aspects, changes in living conditions may be psychologically disturbing; perhaps a parent is an alcoholic or one who is bedridden through a lengthy illness.

Pluto, Ruler of the Ascendant, in Pisces in the Fifth House: There is a strong obsession to "be someone of importance," to express the individuality in a big way through the arts, theater, dancing, photography or writing prose, poetry or detective stories. There is a desire to be the very best and to be recognized as such; however these individuals should not strive to be recognized for themselves but should concentrate on one particular creative talent and become best in that field, thus being recognized for their achievements. This placement can bring unforeseen benefits or loss though speculation, so the natives must be careful of get-rich-quick schemes and con artists who promise immediate financial returns on investments. From the standpoint of children, the natives may adopt or have a child that is sensitive and creative or, in extreme cases, handicapped. These individuals should not put too much trust or faith in love partners who appear illusive or secretive about personal matters as they could be married, secret drinkers or drugs abusers. The natives may experience secret love affairs that will create a dramatic change in their lives, both psychologically and in the personality. This can also indicate a loss or separation from the greatest love of the native's life, which results in the native never seeking another. They may enjoy working with children or teenagers and are interested in their education. There is great sensitivity toward gifted or handicapped children. Women should be careful during pregnancy to avoid certain medication or drugs which may have an effect upon the unborn child or possibly their own health. Anesthetic during delivery could also have a disturbing effect on the unborn child or the mother's health.

Pluto, Ruler of the Ascendant, in the Fifth House in Aries: Pluto entered Aries on April 16, 1822 and left the sign on February 13, 1853. It enters again on June 18, 2066 and leaves on March 10, 2097. Pluto in Aries gives a taste for adventure with a good deal of self-confidence. Because the energies may be totally committed to a loved one it is important to see that this dedication is directed toward someone worthy and deserving of the native. There may be impulsiveness and a lack of restraint in matters of romance, which need to be held in check as there is the capacity to go to extremes. The nature is dynamic, sensual and domineering, and the natives may have to continually regenerate the image they project, especially with close relationships. There is a desire to attain success in life at all costs, and sometimes there is a drastic or radical change of circumstances involving a love relationship in which separation or departure results. Relationships with children may undergo a change for better or worse, depending on aspects to Pluto.

Pluto, Ruler of the Ascendant, in the Sixth House in Aries: There is the ability to act decisively, both independently and in cooperation with others as well as coworkers. These individuals are pioneers, making new discoveries and initiating new projects through their line of work. This placement can lead to obsessional tendencies, dictatorship or rule by force, and those the natives contact through work-related matters. There is a desire to bring other people under the rule of the native. Violent disputes and quarrels are possible with coworkers and bosses. Injuries or accidents at work are possible, and these natives tend to be aggressive and bossy with those in their employ or with whom they work. They should be selective when engaging in sexual contact as sexually transmitted diseases are possible. These individuals are accident prone, not necessarily as a result of their own rashness or lack of caution but because they are drawn to others who fail in this respect. The accent is on combativeness and aggressiveness, so it may be wise for these individuals to work alone or for themselves.

Pluto, Ruler of the Ascendant, in Taurus in the Sixth House: Pluto entered Taurus on May 20, 1851 and left on April 18, 1884. These individuals are thoughtful and considerate, wanting to help others or at least feel as though they are helpful. They feel the disruption of peace and harmony in the working environment, and this external turmoil can affect their health psychologically. There are good powers of concentration and they love working with beautiful objects, gardening, flower arranging and art in various forms. Sometimes there is a compulsive attempt to influence or control others unduly though the bonds of love, giving of gifts or money. Surgery may be required to correct a thyroid problem, remove a cyst from the jaw or neck area, or a goiter. The fixity of this sign can give way to a high degree of intensity that can work on the emotions and lead to high blood pressure, stroke or heart problems. Sometimes an obscure illness may be related to negative psychological causes or the natives may be hypochondriacs who continue to run from one doctor to another seeking impossible cures.

Pluto, Ruler of the Ascendant, in the Seventh House in Taurus: The affections are capable of being deeply stirred, and love for the marriage partner is usually based on strong passions. Sometimes this placement is indicative of a Karmic marriage. There is a capacity for loving intensely, so any emotional relationship may be given greater significance than actually indicated. The sensitive side of these natives is strongly developed and they do not take rejection lightly. They tend to be dogmatic and aggressive in personal behavior and anti-social in marriage relationships and in dealings with the public. A domineering attitude will naturally cause resentment and lead to inharmonious relationships and a battle of the wills. With hard aspects there is the possibility that harsh behavior in marriage may occur through a difficult partner, and they may experience compulsive and painful emotional problems with close love relations. Pluto can also promote emotional upheavals and crises in the marital relationship. Sometimes there are long periods of loneliness and exclusivity due to lack of communication or understanding with the spouse or partner.

Pluto, Ruler of the Ascendant, in the Seventh House in Gemini: Pluto entered Gemini on July 21, 1882 and left the sign on May 25, 1914. Because the mind is sensitive, the power of the idea becomes very compelling and these people can become indoctrinated or may attempt to indoctrinate others in marriage, business or public contacts. At times these individuals may appear to be remote and unreachable because their mental attributes are on a higher dimension of thought. This can be a highly critical placement and, as a result, difficult for marriage. These natives tend to fret, fuss and concern themselves with insignificant details and in the process they try to redo the circumstances in which they find themselves. Due to the dualistic nature of this sign, there can be more than one marriage or the subsequent remarriage of people who have been divorced or separated. These natives may attempt to remake or change certain conditions surrounding close relationship when in reality it is themselves they should remake or change. They may experience divorce or litigation of various kinds.

Pluto, Ruler of the Ascendant, in Gemini in the Eighth House: These individuals may have one of two problems: either a mental hangup on sex or a preoccupation with sexual matters. Much depends on the condition of the third house ruler, planets therein and Mercury by house, sign and aspects thereto. There is a desire to bring other people under the rule of their will, and there may be an inclination toward mental manipulation of others and toward insisting that others change themselves according to the native's sense of values. The altering or changing of documents, wills or insurance policies may provide the backdrop for experiencing mutual financial gain or loss. The death of a sibling or other close family member may change or alter their mental attitude toward life and death.

Pluto, Ruler of the Ascendant, in the Eighth House in Cancer: Pluto entered Cancer on September 10, 1912 and left the sign on February 7, 1939. This placement endows an active subconscious mind with a phenomenal memory of past events and the ability to draw upon these events as a guide for future occurrences. There is strong psychic ability when it comes to intuiting other people's thoughts and feelings, and they may experience prophetic dreams or disturbing nightmares. Emotionally sensitive concerning sexual matters, they prefer others to make the first overture to ensure against any possibility of rejection. They are likely to inherit property from a parent, and the loss or departure of someone will make a major change in the emotional factor in the home or family lifestyle. There is success in legacies and the ability to gain extra funds through the resources of others.

Pluto, Ruler of the Ascendant, in the Ninth House in Cancer: Feelings and instincts are intensified to produce a high degree of sensitivity. The desire nature is strong but the ninth house placement of Pluto leans toward religious convictions and high moral standards that enable the natives to keep their emotional desires under control. There can be a great awareness of crowd atmosphere and the ability to pick up the emotional states of large groups of people. This capacity is useful for those who need to sense what the public is feeling and to evoke a response from the audience. Lecturers, instructors, politicians, radio and television journalists, and motivational promoters have this placement.

There is a possible inheritance of property or possessions through a parent living in a distant city or through a parent-in-law. People with this configuration sometimes feel it is necessary to change their locality, to move to a different environment and begin life anew either to get away from what they feel is a stagnant condition or to separate from a trying emotional relationship. With hard aspects, legal entanglements may result in bankruptcy or loss of property.

Pluto, Ruler of the Ascendant, in the Ninth House in Leo: Pluto entered Leo on October 7, 1937 and left the sign on June 10, 1958. Leo represents the will to create and achieve, and Pluto in this sign adds strong willpower and the ability to achieve or create on a grand scale. These individuals do well in the entertainment field or working in mass media as radio or television announcers or journalists. This placement of Pluto usually adds height to the stature with an upright comportment, a dramatic flair to the personality and, in some cases, intellectual snobbery. Self-confidence and high aims can result from this combination, which is often the sign of a born leader or one who is placed in a position where it is necessary to demonstrate leadership qualities. There may be separation from children who move away to distant cities, and in the case of divorce, legal action may enforce child support or payment of college tuition. Others may attempt to seek legal custody of children. A great deal of travel is a possibility and the natives are likely to come in contact with people from all walks of life. Whether they relocate depends on the condition of the fifth house, the rulers thereof and the planets therein and also the Sun by house, sign and aspects. Some relocate to be near their children who have moved to a distant city. Others move to escape from child support or from an overly possessive love relationship that has outworn its usefulness. Still others move to be near a casino and where there are many nightclubs and entertainment. They may change religious concepts.

Pluto, Ruler of the Ascendant, in the Tenth House in Leo: Sometimes these natives have a compulsive insistency that urges them to act out of self-interest and this may become ever more intense, giving way to unpopularity or an unprofitable business sense. This type of situation will continue until the natives realize they are landing themselves in trouble by consistently giving way to their less creditable impulses. After a time they may be compelled to undertake some kind of self-transformation, not so much out of a desire to become a better person but to avoid placing themselves in uncomfortable predicaments and to improve their business reputation or public image. They have dreams of grandeur and may be overly ambitious, perhaps to compensate for an oversized inferiority complex. There is often resentment against those in authority and an overwhelming, driving ambition to establish themselves as outstanding in some way that will be recognized by others. Women with this placement may achieve this effect by dressing dramatically and seductively to impart an air of sensuality which often attracts the opposite sex and brings them recognition; yet many may feel repulsed by this sort of attention. They can be domineering, dictatorial, possessive and protective of loved ones, especially their offspring. In some cases these natives may even attempt to live their lives through their children, making their decisions or selecting their career choices and never letting their children experience any of the difficult pitfalls that are a part of daily living. They have tremendous leadership powers and will not tolerate being controlled by others; for this reason they should be self-employed or seek a vocation where they will be placed in a management capacity.

Pluto, Ruler of the Ascendant, in the Tenth House in Virgo: Pluto entered Virgo on October 20, 1956 and left the sign on July 29, 1972. There is a great need for self-expression on the mental level, and these individuals can become so mesmerized by ideas and details which are important to them and their careers that they become completely engulfed. They can almost hypnotize themselves into a state of one-pointedness in the pursuit of that which they earnestly desire. Because of this intensive power it is important that they become gripped by the right obsession and do not get lost in any form of exclusivity. There is shrewd appreciation of what the public needs and an awareness of how to best serve them. Analytical traits will be emphasized, making them suitable for occupations such as the medical field, physical therapist, paramedic, veterinarian, secretary, bookkeeper, police officer or firefighter.

Pluto, Ruler of the Ascendant, in the Eleventh House in Virgo: There may be a desire to undertake radical reforms in connection with groups of people, and there is usually great skill in debate, especially when they feel standards are being challenged. These natives tend to be somewhat dogmatic in their approach as a result of having developed a number of firm convictions over the years. Capable of prolonged research, they work best in the scientific field, but gamblers and detectives are not uncommon. Sometimes there is a regimental action in which organizations or employment require the wearing of a uniform as a symbol of unified discipline. These natives should be selective of friends made through work as they can exercise a controlling influence. As this is the second house of money of the tenth house of business, it would be prudent for these natives to keep very good books for the Internal Revenue Service in case of an audit and not to overextend themselves financially.

Pluto, Ruler of the Ascendant, in the Eleventh House in Libra: Pluto entered Libra on October 5, 1971 and left the sign on August 27, 1984. There is a compulsion to be accepted by other people and to participate in cooperative group and social activities. There are certain fixed ideas regarding relationships that have to be changed in order for rebirth to take place in the area of achieving the ultimate hopes and desires. These natives should be wary of overpowering close ties and friends, and should learn to rely on themselves for the fulfillment of their goals. Their deepest hopes can be fulfilled only if they encompass an entire personal transformation. The actions of friends can exert a powerful influence in business or marriage partnerships. How this will work out is indicated by the condition of the seventh house of partnerships, the ruler thereof and planets therein, along with natal Venus by sign, house and aspects thereto. These individuals may establish close relationships with friends of the spouse and extreme care should be taken if these friends are of the opposite sex as emotions can get out of control and possibly lead to extramarital affairs.

Pluto, Ruler of the Ascendant, in the Twelfth House in Libra: This is an unsettling position that can bring danger of intrigue through clandestine affairs. Secret enemies may attempt to create suspicion through anonymous phone calls or letters, yet make it difficult to pinpoint the individual causing the trouble. Deep-rooted psychological problems may result through a difficult relationship, the marriage partner or the opposite sex. There is a tendency to suppress or oppress others. These natives may attempt to attain success through secretive or possibly ruthless means. Some are able to exert a subtle and far reaching influence on their environment, and they must continually regenerate the image they project, especially in connection with relationships.

Pluto, Ruler of the Ascendant, in the Twelfth House in Scorpio: These natives tend to have an impersonal and universal attitude toward life and even toward themselves. A deep-rooted psychological problem may transform their emotions, causing them to withdraw into themselves. This psychological hurt may require long periods of loneliness and abstention from sex and social interaction, for dealing with people often has the troublesome effect of stirring up old emotional hurt that the person is trying to transcend. Some individuals with this placement may suffer an injury or illness that forces them to claim Social Security benefits, Worker's Compensation or other mutually funded income.

Sagittarius Ascendant

Mutable   Fire
Positive   Ruler: Jupiter

Sagittarius is the Jupiter-ruled sign of the natural ninth house and represents honesty, integrity and higher education. Sagittarians are perpetual students, always searching for new subjects of interest.

Character Traits

The majority of Sagittarius rising individuals are easygoing, friendly and jovial with a love for the outdoors, sports and animals. Youth often dread the thought of school because of the confinement that prevents their restless nature from the freedom of exploring the outdoors. In adults, this restlessness leans toward personal independence, an outdoor job or one where there is freedom of movement and action. They cannot stand being tied down to a desk job or to one particular, monotonous machine all day long, but will do so if necessary.

They are highly intelligent with a witty sense of humor. The approach to life is straightforward and they are impetuous and friendly, but feelings are extremely sensitive and they are easily humiliated when criticized by others. They meet people easily, but want to know the mainspring of their actions.

When Sagittarians sell a commodity, they always have to state why someone should buy it. They are better ambassadors than salesmen.

These individuals have good intuition, and try to learn and understand the basic principles that underlie everything in the universe. They collect data and put it into theories, systems or laws, and like to discover the reason for mechanical parts and why businesses are running on a particular line.

Sagittarians are open, honest and forthright in their manner of speech and often have "hoof in mouth disease"—speaking without forethought. Then they get very upset when they discover they have hurt someone's feelings through one of their honest statements. If you want to hear the truth and not what someone thinks you want to hear, ask a Sagittarius.

They have expansive minds, love to learn new things and are bright, curious and love to travel. Some are sports minded (avid television football, golf or boxing fans), and some are firm believers in exercise.

Their love of personal freedom can cause problems in a marriage if the partner does not respect their need for independence.

They are likely to undertake new studies, or keep in touch with happenings around the world. People from other cultures or religions, in-laws or those connected with the judicial system will touch their lives in one way or another.

Sagittarians meet their detractors face-to-face, saying "How come?" They are straight shooters, abhorring underhanded tactics or deceit, preferring to keep their cards on the table.

They can be very generous financially with those who need assistance, and women with this rising sign are casual dressers, preferring designer jeans and Scandinavian sweaters.

Physical Appearance

Individuals possess some Sagittarius qualities and physical features if they have any of the following configurations in the natal chart:
- Sagittarius rising
- Natal Jupiter in the first house (noticeably strong if conjunct the Ascendant)
- Natal Jupiter within orb of aspect of the Ascendant's degree
- Ruler of the first house cusp in Sagittarius
- Ruler of the first house cusp conjunct or otherwise in close aspect with Jupiter
- Sun or Moon in Sagittarius
- Sun or Moon in close aspect with Jupiter
- Sagittarius intercepted in the first house

Sagittarius rising individuals possess one or more of the following features:
- Generally tall and slender with long limbs and a tendency for stooping shoulders
- Unlike the Leo, whose receding hairline starts at the middle of the forehead, Sagittarius hair begins to recede at the temples on each side of the forehead, leaving a tuft in the center until the top is gradually lost to baldness; women usually have high foreheads and

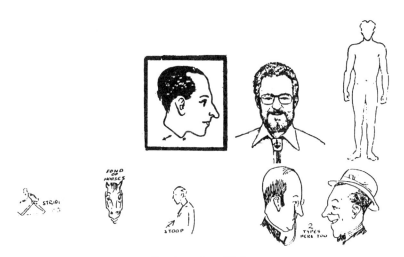

Sagittarius Rising

- many wear bangs to soften the features and shorten the face
- Some have long legs and are fat walkers; because Jupiter rules the hips, women sometimes get what are termed "saddle-bags" or large thighs and hips
- Boys and even men often shuffle or scrape their feet when they walk
- Often tilts the head to one side or bends forward slightly when conversing
- Men have large hands and feet
- Clean-cut, outdoor, sporty looking
- Nose is long, well-proportioned and slightly humped aquiline type

Mentality

Clue Words: Honest, frank, outspoken, curious, direct, optimistic

The Sagittarius mind cannot tolerate details and monotonous tasks. They are not inclined to worry, for their outlook is very optimistic. An insatiable curiosity drives them to seek out the whys and wherefores, and they are frank and open in their manner of speech, but can become angry when anyone questions their integrity. If their excellent intuition goes unheeded, they often regret it later. They may stutter, only because they talk too fast in an effort to get their ideas across, but they have little regard for what others think of them and seldom hold a grudge.

Romantic Inclinations

Clue Words: Tender, affectionate, sociable, generous, impulsive

Sagittarians give the impression that they are highly sexed because of their affectionate and flirtatious nature; actually they are seeking variety in their relationships. They need complete freedom to come and go as they please and will not tolerate being bossed, possessed or restrained by the opposite sex. Preferred partners are either of the same intellectual level or from cultures, religions and backgrounds vastly different from their own.

Health

These natives can maintain good health through regular exercise in the open air, especially if it is combined with a sporting activity such as golf, horseback riding, racquetball or tennis. Some may have claustrophobia, fear of enclosed places, and fear of being alone because their friendly nature needs and seeks out the company of others. The vulnerable areas for health are the hips, thighs and liver. They require a great deal of rest due to slow recuperative powers.

Ascendant Ruler in Signs and Houses

Jupiter, Ruler of the Ascendant, in the First House in Sagittarius: Their clean-cut, sporty, outdoor appearance makes these natives easy to spot as having Jupiter in the first house. They are generally tall, and may put on weight in later years because they tend to overdo the good stuff, which leads to obesity. They are honest and forthright in their manner, humane, sympathetic, honorable, sincere, devout and cheerful. Judgment is good and the intellect is quick, but they lack system and method. These individuals may have troubles in married life due to their love of independence and freedom. They are generous individuals who may be inclined to go overboard at times due to excessive enthusiasm, and will sacrifice much for their fellow man. Success in life depends on their own efforts, and they incline toward religious or philosophical interests. The viewpoint is positive and there is a willingness to meet others half way. They abhor underhanded tactics, deceit and backbiting. There is popularity with the general public and they may have leadership qualities. They can be fortunate through matters connected with travel, export-import or mass communications—radio, television or newspapers—literature, published material, lecturing, teaching, in-laws, legal matters and people of foreign background, other races or cultures or living in distant places. They are usually fond of horses, and may gamble or take risks. Jupiter is the planet of luck and protection and will go a long way in safeguarding these natives against serious accidents and difficult periods in life. Even when hardships appear, they have enough optimism and faith to overcome them. These individuals are quick to take advantage of all opportunities that seem to turn up automatically.

For those who do not inherit a lot of money, they will have the ability to earn money easily. It gives the Midas Touch that brings funds in when they are on their last dollar. Lovers of outdoor sports, animals and especially horses, this placement gives good executive and leadership ability that fits the native for important positions in educational, business or social circles.

Jupiter, Ruler of the Ascendant, in Capricorn in the First House: The mentality is serious, thoughtful and deliberate, and these natives are good organizers who prefer to plan ahead, leaving nothing to chance. The nature is constructive, capable and creative, and they place great importance on attaining higher education. Thoughtful individuals, but quietly compelling in their outlook on life, they are industrious and persevering, firm in their intentions. Capricorn generally promises financial gain, success and happiness later in life, usually after age thirty. This is an excellent placement for outdoor contracting and construction work, real estate, installing garages and, in some cases, public or government careers. Parents, bosses or older people may be more fortunate and of assistance in promoting occupational interests. These natives are careful planners, good organizers and conscientious in their handling of responsible duties. Unlike Jupiter in Sagittarius, these individuals are more reliable with routine matters and apt to pay closer attention to details.

Jupiter, Ruler of the Ascendant, in the Second House in Capricorn: These individuals can obtain financial security through careful and conservative planning. They can be excellent fund managers as they know how to get their money's worth. Utterly fair and just in business and monetary dealings, they expect honest and honorable treatment in return and will not do repeat business with anyone whom they feel has fleeced them. There is possible financial or property gain through in-laws or other figures of authority, and financial talent and the ability to accumulate wealth are frequently marked characteristics of this placement. There is a certain degree of integrity, prestige and authority that wins them the respect they deserve and helps to promote financial endeavors. They are likely to benefit through such matters as law, insurance, real estate, education, lottery, football pools, check pools at work, raffles, Worker's Compensation, Social Security, unemployment benefits or city employment. Sometimes extra funds are earned through added benefits, such as extra pay for working the night shift or dental benefit coverage.

Jupiter, Ruler of the Ascendant, in the Second House in Aquarius: A certain intuitive quality is often present and serves as a warning signal of financial loss. This can be very protective if the individuals have the good sense to follow their intuition. Originality in inventive ideas can be productive of gain through new, unique or innovative endeavors. This placement gives great sensitivity to the needs of others, and they can gain income through astrology, the occult, scientific fields, computers, engineering, radar and electronics. Financial benefits can be had through friends or clubs and organizations, and they can earn income through the handling of funds belonging to clubs and organizations, unions or group-related activities. This placement does not bring steady income, but rather many ups and downs with periods of plenty followed by periods of lean. Usually people who are paid on a commission basis, rather than a weekly paycheck, have this placement. Nevertheless, Jupiter protects through lucky, unexpected and last minute refunds that arrive just when they are short of funds. There is also the possibility of handling funds for religious or charitable organizations.

Jupiter, Ruler of the Ascendant, in the Third House in Aquarius: The mentality is forceful, unconventional and determined, with originality of thought and an interesting or unique logic and manner of reasoning. There is a great love of personal independence and freedom of speech, and an element of luck in travel. These individuals may have an unusual, bizarre or witty sense of humor and love to make shocking and way-out statements so they can observe the effect they have on others. They usually have a dynamic, magnetic way of speaking that holds the attention of their audience. Possibly a bit peculiar, eccentric, and curious, this placement gives the ability to study deep and profound subjects such as metaphysics, astrology, computers, engineering, electronics, law, philosophy or religion. They are independent in thought and are not influenced by the opinions of others. Always eager to investigate unusual fields of interest, travel, correspondence and education may be important factors in personality development. Some are likely to travel with friends or groups of people to attend seminars to exchange ideas and viewpoints. They seek friendships with group activities of intellectual interest. A brother or sister may suddenly move to a distant city, and a sibling may be a borderline genius or have a muscular or nervous disability. Jupiter provides good protection against accidents; for example, if a prankster removes a barrier from an uncovered manhole during the evening hours, these natives will intuitively sense the need to stop the car immediately and then discover the gaping hole in the street.

Jupiter, Ruler of the Ascendant, in the Third House in Pisces: The nature is studious, quiet, unassuming, sociable and kind. Because this is a mutable planet in a mutable sign in a mutable house these natives can be restless, changeable and have great difficulty concentrating on one particular subject long enough to digest it thoroughly. What they learn and pick up in the way of knowledge is through their psychic or intuitive ability. Some are mediumistic with a capacity for visualization—seeing in their mind's eye what they want to achieve and then going after it. These natives love to read write or study the strange and the supernatural. Studies are associated with psychology, art, poetry, music and the occult or metaphysics. They are naturally generous with an inclination to help others. These individuals must guard against the tendency to daydream or drift while traveling as they generally have more than one subject, project or errand on their minds and instead of concentrating on traffic conditions let their minds wander over the multitude of things they have to do. It is important to be careful when signing papers or making statements, and legal action may result through neighbors, possibly connected with chemicals in the water that seep into the yard from emptying a pool. There is danger of accidents while traveling due to ice on the roads or misty rain and foggy conditions that make for poor visibility. Legal action could be tied in some way with a brother or sister.

Jupiter, Ruler of the Ascendant, in the Fourth House in Pisces: These individuals are not eager to make sacrifices for others or to do things for them without knowing the full details of the problem involved. This is good, for it will go a long way toward stopping people in their environment who may try to impose or take unfair advantage of them. They must avoid impulsive actions, doing things on the spur of the moment. This placement increases the emotions and the imagination. There may be a strong interest in psychic research and the occult. Living lazy lives of ease, they prefer to stay at home and listen to music or watch television, causing them to seek isolation and exclusivity. They need a country cottage or a trailer near a pond or body of water for inner peace, relaxation and escapism from the trials and tribulations of life. Legal issues concerning property may involve sewer problems, fumes, gas leakage, asbestos or fraudulent construction materials. When buying or purchasing a home or property, they should read and understand the fine print for possible escape clauses. There is the possibility that they may have to take legal steps to have a parent or parent-in-law committed to a nursing home.

Jupiter, Ruler of the Ascendant, in the Fourth House in Aries: Judgment and material considerations are apt to be made quickly and on the basis of what is evident at the moment. These individuals seldom do much prolonged pondering on actions they will or will not take, but incline strongly to make their decisions immediately and take for granted their ability to cope with any unforeseen developments along the way. Their response to new situations being immediate and definite, they develop a state of consciousness in which they depend primarily on their own abilities. Because there will be little time between their decisions and the actions taken in new situations, they are unable to call upon the services of family members. In other words, they are more apt to be the decisive members of the family or, if female, the ones who may wear the "pants" in the family. Family members and others in the immediate environment are extremely likely to take the Sagittarius' word for things, and sometimes, owing to their evident sincerity, decide to abide by the opinions or policies of the native rather than argue an issue, which often strikes them as a waste of time. The domestic environment is frequently of great importance and home conditions play an important part in shaping the character. There is a dislike of routine and being under another's authority, and there is a greater chance of luck and success through material prosperity as life advances. There is a possibility of litigation and disputes over property, or disputes with in-laws, or they may require surgery or suffer an accident.

Jupiter, Ruler of the Ascendant, in the Fifth House in Aries: The character analysis is the same as the previous paragraph. There is success and luck through creative and personal endeavors, and these natives can be impetuous and impatient in love affairs. Either sex may be attracted to those of a different culture, nationality, background or religion. This is an excellent placement for a sportsman or gym instructor. They may become involved in lawsuits through and accidents connected with places of amusement, nightclubs, sports, health spas, theaters, schools or racetracks. Men usually are drawn toward influential, distinguished ladies and those of foreign or intellectual background. Women are drawn toward professionals, merchants or those in good financial or social standing. With hard aspects, women can be attracted to men of a different race or color, or have clandestine affairs with priests. This can be a good placement for speculation connected with foreign products, exports/imports, instruments and products made of steel.

Jupiter, Ruler of the Ascendant, in the Fifth House in Taurus: This is a good placement for Jupiter because these individuals are fixed in their opinions, reserved, affectionate and generous. The judgment is generally sound and reliable with emphasis on material things and the accumulation of money because they love the creature comforts. They are not chance takers and are less inclined to gamble, but they may benefit financially or receive expensive gifts from romantic partners or games of chance such as football pools, bingo, lottery or raffles. Legal affairs may surround the affairs of children, not necessarily their own, and either be a source of financial drain or gain. These individuals have a natural flair for successful speculation as a result of their conservative and sound approach to handling money matters. They do well in real estate, construction or the building trades, and there are benefits through schools, creative hobbies and places of entertainment. Being a fixed sign, there is little desire for change once they select the object of their affection, and they are drawn to romantic partners of influence both in business and finances. Lottery and raffle wins are more likely to occur after age thirty. They should consider entering the entertainment world as Jupiter in Taurus often endows a marvelous singing voice unless Jupiter has many hard aspects. They can be collectors of beautiful objects, jewelry or paintings.

Jupiter, Ruler of the Ascendant, in the Sixth House in Taurus: The general characteristics are the same as the above paragraph. This increases sound business judgment due to practical application of organizational abilities, and is less extravagant than other signs unless under hard aspects. Money is spent on equipment to improve production and even then these natives are cautious in the selection of new machinery, computers and office supplies. Discreet and discriminating in the discharge of their duties, they sometimes gain new technical knowledge while on the job and receiving a salary. Others may be able to attend college part time with tuition and textbooks paid for by the company. This is one of the most protective places for jupiter in matters connected with health, and in general brings certain illnesses to their attention before they get a firm grip on the natives. This is an excellent placement for bankers, money lenders, cashiers, bookkeepers, payroll clerks, flower arrangers, real estate brokers and most any occupation where methodical handling of detailed tasks must be performed on a daily basis. These individuals have the fortitude and determination to stick with a task no matter how boring it may be. There is the ability to inspire respect and the willing cooperation of subordinate and fellow workers is an important factor in ensuring success. They have the capacity for loyal and dedicated service to the company.

Jupiter, Ruler of the Ascendant, in the Sixth House in Gemini: Jupiter in Gemini is far different from Jupiter in Taurus. There is a restlessness and changeability that won't stand for routine tasks and boring details unless absolutely necessary. These natives require a vocation where there is freedom of movement and decision, as they thrive on change and do not do well in a position with too much fixity in the routine. This is an excellent placement for people who work with their minds or their hands—not manual labor, but something that requires skill and cleverness such as a mail order business, bookstore, video store, computer business, auto parts store, publishing firm or operating a printing press. They may have to learn a foreign language in connection with their employment or be teachers, lecturers, flight attendants, travel agents or salespeople. Sometimes they hold two jobs or become involved in more than one business or enterprise. Optimism and sound reasoning make for good business sense and many feel they are capable of executive leadership or management positions. There is clarity of thought with the capacity to resolve perplexing problems at work with ease. For some, frequent travel to strange places or other countries may be indicated, and they may work with or hire brothers or sisters as employees. The lungs are the most vulnerable part of the body, and there may be bouts with the flu, colds and pneumonia; they should avoid smoking. The liver and the nervous system, as well as tumors in the chest area, need to be watched. With hard aspects, there may be an inability to concentrate on one subject long enough to complete it. Although the mentality is likely to be swift and brilliant, much may not be accomplished if they become entangled in too many projects. In some cases, they may sue a neighbor over matters concerning a dog or cat.

Jupiter, Ruler of the Ascendant, in the Seventh House in Gemini: These natives have a friendly disposition and are courteous and truthful. They are fond of change, travel and mental recreation. They must guard against restlessness, feelings of uncertainty and changeability, and may have good mathematical and literary ability. This is a good placement for public relations, planning social affairs and counseling since these natives are good speakers and have the ability to manipulate situations and people without antagonizing anyone. Much depends on the aspect, but some could have an attraction toward a brother- or sister-in-law. Married life is not easy as work often takes the natives away from home for long periods or there is trouble caused by in-laws. They have to guard against thoughtlessness, and trouble is possible through careless speech or written statements that could result in litigation.

Jupiter, Ruler of the Ascendant, in the Seventh House in Cancer: The emotional nature is deep, and these natives are good humored, benevolent, humane, patriotic and interested in the public welfare. They may inherit property through marriage or in-laws. Although there is a great love for home life, they may have to travel a good deal. There is a deep sense of inner security that comes from great confidence and the need to own a home. Gains are usual through the marriage or business partner, and the marriage partner may be of the May-December type, either vastly younger or older. Some marry someone of a different religion, culture or intellectual background. There is a willingness to cooperate, not only in marriage but also in friendships and partnerships and with associates. Seldom do these individuals divorce because family religious principles usually make divorce impossible or difficult or the individual refuses to divorce out of a fear of losing the home and property. They may gain weight in later years as they are inclined to excess in food and drink. They love to entertain and have small social gatherings in the home.

Jupiter, Ruler of the Ascendant, in the Eighth House in Cancer: There is strong emotional intensity with an interest in deep research of unusual subjects such as astrology, the occult, death and life in the hereafter, and metaphysics. Sometimes dreams have a way of foretelling future events and they should try to remember them and also note the planetary aspects that may have occurred during the sleeping hours. They may have to travel to attend a funeral of a loved one living in a distant city. There is an excellent chance that they will gain property or goods through an inheritance, and good luck and fortune comes through the resources of others. There is possible gain or loss through legal affairs in connection with property or that of a parent or parent-in-law. This is also an excellent placement for real estate and dealing with public commodities and food on a grand scale, such as catering.

Jupiter, Ruler of the Ascendant, in the Eighth House in Leo: These natives have a great deal of willpower, deep emotions, determination and fixity of purpose that does not sway them from their course of action or decision. They think big and do things on a grand scale, desirous of having the best and to be the best in their chosen field; they love power and control and often feel that others should cater to their needs. The powerful will and aggressive tendencies can be both constructive and destructive. People who are obsessed with winning at sporting activities could be targets for possible injury to the eyes, back or heart. Their compulsion to win and to be the best can push them to extremes. Caution is advised to control this inner tension so as to avoid complications with the heart or circulatory system. This placement indicates a mind that is active, analytical and self-confident with excessive pride, ambition and perseverance with fanatical faith in self. Legal issues may involve child support or occur in connection with insurance coverage. Women may suffer miscarriages or difficulties in childbirth, or an in-law may require open heart surgery. Sometimes a promotion to a management position comes as a result of the passing of a supervisor. They are likely to gain through an inheritance, and this placement also increases the chance for winning big in the lottery or through raffles.

Jupiter, Ruler of the Ascendant, in the Ninth House in Leo: One of the best sign placements for Jupiter, it endows fixity to the changeable nature of the planet. These natives are good natured, loyal, courteous, generous, benevolent and compassionate. They have good judgment, wisdom and willpower, which gives them the capacity for positions of trust and responsibility. The mentality is diplomatic and interested in the fine arts and culture. There is luck and good fortune through the mass media, journalism, radio and television, travel, higher education or diplomatic affairs. These individuals are proud of their accomplishments, have lofty ideas and can be intellectual snobs in a nice way. They are never happy in subordinate positions as they are at their best in any management or supervisory position. They carry themselves regally upright and have to be "top dog." Their manner is confident, expansive and proud, often inspiring real hero worship. Legal difficulties may stem through the affairs of children, not necessarily their own. Their children usually want the best in a college education and feel they are entitled to it. In-laws are generally wealthy, prominent or influential in social circles.

Jupiter, Ruler of the Ascendant, in the Ninth House in Virgo: This is not the best placement for Jupiter, a mutable planet in a mutable sign in a mutable house, as it increases the potential for restlessness and changeability. Travel for work purposes is conducive to gain. This configuration strengthens the efficient, practical and discriminating side of the nature, yet at the same time adds a tendency to be somewhat critical and faultfinding when errors occur. There is less tolerance with this placement for people who make mistakes and hard feelings can result if one continues to criticize or demand perfection. Relocation may be necessary for improvement of health or the occupation may require frequent travel. In-laws may be chronically ill, critical or demanding. Sometimes a lawsuit results through conditions surrounding domestic pets, through an accident or illness as a result of working conditions or discrimination due to race, gender or age.

Jupiter, Ruler of the Ascendant, in the Tenth House in Virgo: This is a far better placement for Jupiter because it is an earth house. There is practical and conscientious application toward business and the working environment. The natives have good moral standards, and there is more control of natural restlessness and desire for change. These individuals require fair recognition for their efforts and services; if they are treated unfairly, they take independent steps to seek improvement of their situation. Status and reputation in the career are very important and they strive to hold fast to their honorable public image. There is usually some connection with the armed forces or working for the city, state or federal government. This placement is excellent for those interested in the medical field, accounting, engineering and occupations requiring careful handling and discharge of details, and is likely to bring the native in touch with people from all walks of life in connection with the occupation.

Jupiter, Ruler of the Ascendant, in the Tenth House in Libra: The disposition is mild, sincere, kind, sociable and obliging, and the native is a lover of peace and harmony, justice and all intellectual and cultural pursuits. These individuals are attracted to the public and social side of life, and the occupation tends to bring material prosperity, social prestige and nobility of character. From time to time, they may be placed in positions in which they have to act as go-betweens or mediators, helping others to seek compromise. The forming of a partnership in a business enterprise can be productive of gain or loss depending on the aspects Jupiter receives in the natal chart and through major transits at the time of consideration. If partnerships do exit, it is important that these natives be the dominant partners for they are likely to rebel against restriction toward independent decisions. Due to their easygoing, friendly and sociable manner, they can easily become involved in clandestine relationships through their place of employment; either one or both of the parties may be married, which makes for a difficult relationship. For women, it is wise to avoid such associations with bosses or other figures of authority as harmony in the working environment may be difficult to maintain. Becoming involved in a sticky divorce case can harm the reputation and professional standing in the community. This is one of the best placements for judges, attorneys, mediators, counselors and those who deal with art in any form.

Jupiter, Ruler of the Ascendant, in the Eleventh House in Libra: This is a lucky house for Jupiter because it can bring success and achievement of the natives' fondest hopes and desires. Social affairs and organizational activities bring contacts leading to the forming of influential friends and associations. The natives may form legal partnerships with friends or work in collaboration with them on a mutual endeavor. This placement generally signifies male friends; however, due to its marriage implications, the natives may meet people at social functions which, if the friendships develop into emotional or romantic alliances, could have disturbing repercussions on the marital state. These individuals do not like to travel alone and are more likely to take a companion along or travel with guided tours. Creature comforts are of utmost importance and only the better class hotels will do when they travel if they can afford them. This is an excellent placement for social directors, travel agents, marriage counselors and public relations workers for conventions and large gatherings.

Jupiter, Ruler of the Ascendant, in the Eleventh House in Scorpio: These natives possess a secretive nature and seldom reveal anything of their personal lives or finances. There is strong emotional intensity with the ability to control their emotions. They are extremely loyal to their friends and expect the same treatment in return, although they seldom reveal their innermost feelings to them; when they do, and if the trust is betrayed, Scorpios never forgive or forget and, once hurt, can be utterly vindictive and sarcastic. At times, feelings of resentment are not easy to overcome and can create friction and animosity between close ties. Friends and social or cultural groups or clubs are important and these natives may one day have a controlling influence as officers for a club or organization. There is the possibility of inheritance or material gain through the demise of a friend, and this is also an excellent placement for unexpected windfalls that can fulfill the natives' fondest hopes and wishes.

Jupiter, Ruler of the Ascendant, in the Twelfth House in Scorpio: This is a far better placement for Jupiter in Scorpio than the eleventh house as Scorpio has greater affinity with water houses. There is a high degree of emotional sensitivity, especially toward conditions in the immediate environment, and there is excellent psychic or intuitive ability and the capacity to sink deep into research projects. These natives make good trouble shooters, individuals who must ferret out troubling situations and come to the root of the problem. This configuration may be found in the charts of plumbers and electricians who have to determine where, along the line (plumbing or electricity) the root of the problem lies. There may be a strong interest in hypnosis, self-healing or healing with the hands, the medical or surgical field, detective work and engineering. Deep, intense secrecy is still present but not in the degree of revenge found with Jupiter in Scorpio in the eleventh house. These individuals are more inclined to believe that the universal being will take care of their enemies: "what goes around, comes around" is one of their strongest beliefs. They also say, "God will take care of them for me," and when they hear an enemy has had an accident, they like to remark, "See, I told you God would take care of them for me." Jupiter in Scorpio in the twelfth house is helpful for interest in hospitals, institutions, prison reform, criminology and the occult or metaphysical. People who listen to troubles and secrets of others usually have this placement, such as bartenders, psychologists and counselors.

Jupiter, Ruler of the Ascendant, in the Twelfth House in Sagittarius: With the ruling planet in the twelfth house, these natives always have to maintain a strong sense of integrity and honesty and keep all situations, circumstances and companions above board. Jupiter in the twelfth house can work either for or against; much depends on how the natives apply the energy of that planet. There may be a reclusive tendency along with excellent creative work. Success comes through study, research and possibly the medical field or through work for the police department. Loss of prestige can result from an overzealous religious attitude or engaging in unethical or illegal activities. Jupiter in the twelfth house in Sagittarius provides a good degree of protection against accidents and possible gain through lawsuits due to hospital or medical treatments as a result of an automobile accident.

Capricorn Ascendant

Cardinal   Earth
Passive   Ruler: Saturn

Capricorn is a Saturn-ruled sign of the nature of the tenth house, which is the house of responsibility, perseverance, ambition and career. For this reason it is natural for a native with Capricorn on the Ascendant to be more concerned with the achievement of public recognition and a high position in the community or within the framework of their abilities.

Character Traits

Capricorn is an earth sign, so these natives perceive reality through practical and materialistic matters. Saturn is the ruler of Capricorn; its main source of energy is to limit expansion so that energy can be focused and defined in one's personal affairs. Capricorns are active due to the cardinal element, and the earth sign makes them practical. They are the doers and the achievers of the zodiac. Capricorn governs what is open and apparent to all. These natives are ambitious, as the sign governs the professional and public life. Capricorns demand facts and can become exasperated with anyone who continually cries for emotional support and affection. They also demand efficiency and are good organizers.

Capricorn natives collect, seize and hold things because they increase their value in the eyes of the world. When something is worn out it will be replaced with something finer and better. Capricorns prefer one or two highly prized suits or dresses that are well-made, well-cut and correct in every detail. They are generally self-sufficient. They do not want nor ask for help, but are ever seeking people of high social standing so they can obtain help or assistance from them. They are possessed with a strong will and a great deal of patience.

The character is persevering and enduring. Cautious and secretive, and often suspicious of the motives of others, they sometimes are loners and are slow to make friends. Capricorns are not afraid of hard work, and are reliable and disciplined. Being very goal oriented, they can delay immediate pleasure for long-term gain. They have the ability to stick with tasks that would overwhelm the average individual, yet are sensitive and take rejection personally. They want to be admired and looked up to. Although they are quite serious, they also possess a dry, witty sense of humor and can be delightful to have around. As Capricorn is the natural tenth house sign, these natives are business people and practical appliers of ideas and plans if, in their judgment, they are valuable. They are conservative, full of pride in their achievements and dislike physical combat.

Physical Appearance

Individuals will possess some of the Capricorn qualities and physical features if they have any of the following configurations in the natal chart:
- Capricorn rising
- Saturn in the first house (noticeably stronger if conjunct the Ascendant)
- Saturn within orb of the Ascendant's degree
- Ruler of the first house (other than Saturn) in Capricorn
- Ruler of the first house conjunct or otherwise in close aspect with Saturn
- Sun or Moon in Capricorn
- Sun or Moon in close aspect with Saturn
- Capricorn intercepted in the first house

Capricorn rising individuals possess one or more of the following features:
- Average height; usually thin with a bony body, although some are overweight
- Narrow chest, possibly with hunched shoulders
- Sometimes a halting or clumsy way of walking which may be due to lack of balance, problems with the knees or rheumatism in the joints
- Sharp, bony-featured face and the chin sometimes comes to a point
- Pale or shallow skin, forehead relatively low with prominent eyebrows that often protrude over the eyes
- Some have dark circles under the eyes
- Nose is sharp with a dip at the end, indicating acquisitiveness and inquisitiveness, not necessarily personal but very persistent

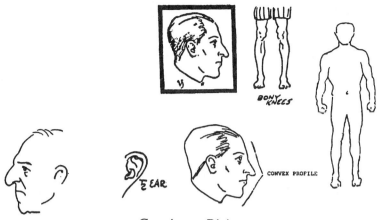

Capricorn Rising

- Mouth usually thin and small
- Weak, small eyes that may tear or water easily, especially with weather changes

Mentality

Clue Words: Cautious, persistent, practical, enduring, ambitious

Conscious of details with a good memory for them, Capricorns are conventional and class conscious, especially if on the way up. They tend to boss and advise others, and love to speak frankly of others' faults while disliking comments about their own. Capricorns like to make a good impression and want credit for what they do. They will remain behind the scenes to handle responsibilities effectively as long as they are known as the power behind the throne. Capricorns want their own way because they think it is the best way and are willing to make others quite uncomfortable for their own good. They possess a dry, witty sense of humor, and do not mince words whether in speech or writing. Hemming and hawing while talking is a guise to gather more time to digest the facts or formulate comments.

Romantic Inclinations

Clue Words: Loyal, reserved, trustworthy, honorable

Capricorn's earth element endows the native with strong sexual drives but seldom are they able to express them with deep emotional feelings. They are deeply sensitive people who fear rejection and ridicule; therefore, they tend to build a wall of reserve and aloofness which may be difficult for the average person to penetrate.

Health

Capricorns have a tendency for frequent colds and chills. They should guard against despondency and depression. The most vulnerable areas for health problems are the skin, bony structure of the body, knees and teeth. There is the possibility of rheumatism or arthritis and hardening of the arteries. They may require dentures or have hearing problems.

Ascendant Ruler in Signs and Houses

Saturn, Ruler of the Ascendant, in the First House in Capricorn: These natives are shy and introverted with a strong concern for practical necessities along with a rather introspective tendency as they redefine their overall approach to life. As children they no doubt preferred the company of older people or adults. Reliability is one of their prominent traits because others come to depend on them and their serious sense of responsibility. No doubt all Capricorn rising people have had their share of burdens and responsibilities that may have started early in their youth. In their determination to be independent, they give others the impression that they do not need affection and may appear aloof or standoffish when in reality they need more love and affection than all the other twelve signs of the zodiac. It seems difficult for them to express their emotions. Perhaps they have hard-working parents who were too busy to fulfill their emotional needs, thus causing them to become loners, sticking with only a few close friends made during their formative school years. They try to fill specific needs from within themselves instead of relying on others to fill them, and as they become more centered and self-sufficient need to rely less on external props and more on their inner resources to provide security. Past experiences pay off in the sense that they are apt to meet their challenges with the advantages gained from past lessons in living and to gain confidence from the success of present endeavors. A strained posture and a slow way of walking are found with some Capricorn rising individuals (to overcompensate for some real or imagined handicap). These natives are often slow healers who suffer prolonged periods of chronic conditions, which can be as simple as common colds or allergies. As Saturn in the first house in Capricorn represents an older person, a grandparent or other figure of authority will have a great influence on the upbringing or conditioning of their psychological patterns.

Saturn, Ruler of the Ascendant, in the First House in Aquarius: Many of the above characteristics will prevail; however, there is the tendency to play the Pied Piper role with younger people as they enjoy having youngsters look up to them as substitute parental figures. During their early years they may have friends who are much younger, and then seem to appreciate older individuals as they mature. Their early environment is not one of a normal family as a grandparent or another older member of the family disturbs the routine with unexpected happenings, either becoming suddenly and unexpectedly ill, going in and out of the hospital at short notice or traveling a great deal, coming in and out of the home at odd intervals. In some instances, friends may bring some degree of obligation or liability into the relationship that may, technically speaking, place them the natives in a parental role to these people. There is usually some degree of unusual talent that the natives should try to promote—scientific, astrology, the occult or creative designs and furniture making. Woodworking projects can be a source of easing their inner tension, and others may discover that meditation or reading is a marvelous outlet for relaxation of inner tension.

Saturn, Ruler of the Ascendant, in the Second House in Aquarius: The general theme is the same as having Saturn in Aquarius in the first house except when it covers finances; in that case there are likely to be periods of plenty followed by periods of lean. Money seems to fluctuate, primarily due to the native's source of income—a cut in overtime hours or unsteady income due to commission sales. These natives love nothing better than to be self-employed so they can work whatever hours they desire and at their own pace. Some natives may be affected by government affiliated affairs connected with money, such as unexpectedly being laid off and having to collect unemployment benefits, or a work-related illness that results in Worker's Compensation. Others may work for the Internal Revenue Service, the state lottery commission, Social Security, etc., and some will have to learn how to operate a computer or other electronic or technical machinery in connection with their job.

Saturn, Ruler of the Ascendant, in the Second House in Pisces: These natives may find it difficult to express themselves in large circles of people or before the world. They should avoid the tendency to dwell in self-pity and refuse to progress financially or materially because of a negative attitude or lack of confidence. A more positive approach brings opportunities to concentrate their efforts in constructive investigations, research, preparations and studies that will enhance earning ability. Moods will vary and sometimes they are more secretive or question their capabilities for achieving various successes. Hidden influences or complex situations may surround their financial picture from time to time, and a parent or a figure of authority may be a source of financial drain or gain, especially through unforeseen circumstances. They often surround themselves with stockpiles of provisions and seldom discard anything once acquired. But, like one prompted by the dread of being without some needed item, they continually ration themselves, making do with less than most in life. And because of strong self-centered interests, they resist sharing which, if unchecked, could result in selfishness and undermine their scene of security and trust. They are practical and down-to-earth, with a healthy respect for established values and seldom, if ever, invest time, energy or cash in anything untried, unproven or questionable. And, even though Saturn may be in the second house of money, its sign position in Pisces is likely to indicate something unusual surrounding the affairs of one parent or possibly both. The native is either orphaned and reared by substitute parents, abandoned by a parent, the parents were divorced and one remarried (giving the native a step-parent), one may have a chronic health problem (and frequently in and out of hospitals) or be a substance abuser (alcohol or drugs.) This is a good placement for those who work in bars or with shoes or leather goods, or are creative in woodworking projects; they can also be psychologists, house painters and musicians. Personal chronic health problems might require medication to keep them under control.

Saturn, Ruler of the Ascendant, in the Third House in Pisces: Feelings and emotions are likely to affect the way you think and, if they are permitted to get out of control, can lead to unreasonable fears and phobias. At times you may find it nearly impossible not only to get your ideas across to people, but also to formulate them in order to make them practically applicable in your day-to-day affairs. When you feel mentally disoriented, uncertain or confused regarding an important decision or subject, try to simplify it and things will become easier to comprehend. Try to develop a perfect balance by applying your mentality to serious, productive endeavors while still enjoying and appreciating the laughter and fun that life has to offer. You may have had difficulty studying and learning difficult subjects during your formative school years. However, as you entered high school you began to realize the importance of higher education and its value toward a productive career. Perhaps it was during this period of time that you discovered your best thinking and studying was accomplished in an atmosphere of isolation and solitude where there was little chance of disturbing interruptions. Your moods will vary from time to time as you tend to become more secretive or begin to question your capabilities for achieving various successes. Increased mental sensitivity can bring you to a point where you will feel you understand something about yourself that you have never before understood. There exists the possibility that you may have a step-brother or step-sister. This placement of Saturn in Pisces in your third house can limit the number of siblings, or you may have one that may be mentally, physically or emotionally impaired.

Saturn, Ruler of the Ascendant, in the Third House in Aries: These natives blow hot and cold when it comes to speaking and writing. When a bill arrives that they believe is in error, their first response is to immediately call the store and tell them what they think of the bookkeeper—until Saturn places a halt to their impetuous actions and instead decides to write a cold, no-nonsense letter calling attention to their mistake and demanding rectification thereof. When it comes to personal affairs, they are quick to arrive at decisions, but when others confront them for an answer, they tend to ponder and make them wait because these natives think others may not listen or take their advice. These Capricorn rising people are cautious communicators, preferring to think through what they want to say before speaking and they always seem to be revising what they write, but they can ad lib if caught in a pinch. They communicate in a clear and meaningful manner and probably have the ability to impart instructional information. The secret with this placement is not to be too impatient with those who do not grasp information as readily as they do. Although they are slow learners when it comes to subject matter that does not interest them personally, the memory is good and they generally retain what has been attained. As the third house governs accidents, these natives should be especially careful around large trucks, buses and vans.

Saturn, Ruler of the Ascendant, in the Third House in Taurus: This is an excellent placement as it tends to add fixity of purpose to Saturn's mentality. You will always ponder very cautiously and carefully when presented with major decisions, especially those that concern the earning or spending of personal finances. However, there will be times when you will lose out on a fantastic monetary offer due to the tendency to evaluate the situation a bit too long, thereby losing out to someone else who grabbed the brass ring far more quickly than you did. You will always be cautious before taking action of any kind as your primary concern will be to safeguard your reputation against anything that may have a negative effect upon your professional career. You are a stubborn person who will stick to your ideals and principles until such a time that someone can clearly illustrate to you why a certain type of action may be better than another. Always be careful that you do not talk and eat at the same time. There exists the possibility that on occasion food can slip down into the windpipe and cause an embarrassing choking situation if you are in a public restaurant. At some point in life you may be placed in the position of having to support or lend money to a brother or sister.

Saturn, Ruler of the Ascendant, in the Fourth House in Aries: It may have been difficult for you to achieve the affection and emotional response that you needed from your parents. No doubt they were good, supportive parents, but they either had to work hard to establish a home life or you may have lost one early in life. As a result of your early environment you have a very disciplined emotional response to situations and those in your environment. This in turn may give others the impression that you are cold, detached and aloof, which is far from the truth because the one thing you need most out of life is to have someone love you. Life has not been easy, with periodic responsibilities and burdens being thrust upon your shoulders such as the necessity of having to rear your children alone or having to care for an ill parent or parent-in-law. There will be a strong inner drive for security at all costs. Owning a home will probably be your number one objective—one with lots of land and trees, not too close to neighbors. As you begin to mature you may discover that it is you who must play the dominant role in the family, making all the important family decisions. The necessity to maintain an adequate home life for your family may force you to seek employment that can be operated from the home base so that you can be there whenever your children need you.

Saturn, Ruler of the Ascendant, in the Fourth House in Taurus: Saturn is not comfortable in the fourth house, being in its fall. As the fourth house represents the grave, Saturn there is a testimony of longevity with these natives generally living to a ripe old age. They prefer a comfortable, neat home that is isolated from or not too close to neighbors, one with a lot of land, trees and shades on the windows to pull down when it suits their mood. Growing up isn't an easy experience, as many are born into disadvantaged family situations where sudden disruptive circumstances may separate them from one of the parents (either through death, a serious illness, divorce or abandonment), forcing the natives to grow up prematurely without the benefit of a normal family existence. The likelihood is great for a conscientious parent who has to work hard to earn and maintain a decent standard of living, but is never there when the native needs him or her the most. Heavy responsibilities are probably forced upon the shoulders of these natives during their formative years, which keeps them from truly enjoying a carefree, happy childhood. These natives keep pretty much to themselves, preferring to keep their personal affairs private; as a rule they remain somewhat of a mystery to family members. Because of their tendency toward personal secrecy, no one ever knows the extent of the emotional cross they have to bear. As they mature, the care and responsibility of a parent or close relative is another burden they have to bear, more through a sense of duty than an attitude of devotion. With soft aspects to Saturn in the fourth house, the natives may gain financially or materially through a parent. This is also an excellent placement for home builders or real estate agents.

Saturn, Ruler of the Ascendant, in the Fourth House in Gemini: The fourth house represents the end of life and Saturn therein often indicates longevity. Thus, individuals with this placement are likely to outlive their brothers and sisters. If you smoke, it would be a good idea to discontinue the habit as soon as possible as Saturn in Gemini can indicate problematic health conditions involving the lungs later in life. There is the possibility that you may one day own two homes or a dual dwelling. It is not advisable to consider joint ownership with a sibling regarding a piece of property or property containing two houses as you are likely to be the one to bear the burden and heavy responsibilities regarding the upkeep and repairs. This placement is often found in charts of people who work from their home or have a profession that requires making frequent telephone calls or handling a lot of paper work in the home. Such would be the case with insurance salesmen and teachers who take papers home to correct and grade. You may, at some point in life, share your home with a parent, grandparent or other older relative such as an aunt or uncle.

Saturn, Ruler of the Ascendant, in the Fifth House: No doubt your parents taught you early in life the value of a savings account and prudence with money, and now you may be trying to instill the same financial virtues into your children. However, they may feel as though you are rather tight with your money and their allowances until the time comes when they mature and have to work for a living. Only then will they appreciate the lessons of thrift that you have tried to teach them. You may do a little investing but your best bet would be government bonds, real estate or CDs as they offer little risk. One thing that you should invest in is your talent for collecting things, especially items that grow in value with age such as stamps, coins and antiques. And ditto for gambling as you are likely to try your hand at the lottery, bingo games or raffle tickets. You won't take chances when it comes to money, but there will be times when you are tempted to try your luck. When you do, you will discover you have come out farther ahead financially than when you started. As a host or hostess you can entertain lavishly to the point where your guests will think that you have spent hours on food preparation, when in reality you are a marvelous organizer, planning everything ahead of time and doing most of the work several days in advance. One thing you detest most is having someone in your kitchen trying to help you when that person is really in the way. You know intuitively where everything is, and as you tend to turn abruptly to reach for something, you are apt to bump into it, which only serves to delay and hinder your precise plan of action. This placement of Saturn often limits the number of children or restricts them altogether.

Saturn, Ruler of the Ascendant, in the Fifth House in Gemini: With Saturn in the fifth house, developments in close relationships exhibit two primary characteristics. First, they are more likely to be evolutionary rather than revolutionary, developing gradually and naturally, rather than through sudden upsets or upheavals. Second, these occur as the result of changes of attitude, priorities and perceptions rather than from changes in the environment or in other people. Independent feelings can create an occasional chafing at the bit when close relationship responsibilities conflict with personal pleasures. They have the ability to bring a personally unique or creative talent, especially in writing, to a new level of development but it requires focus and persistence. As these natives come to a deeper understanding of themselves, their natural abilities flow more easily to the surface of their being. It is important to recognize these talents for what they are, the real essence of the individuality, and they should be nurtured as if tiny seedlings. With time, care and attention, writing ability can blossom into a rewarding and useful means of personal self-expression. The prime concern of these natives with children (not necessarily their own) is education, as they put great value on the attainment of knowledge and, through it, a higher position in life. The affairs of children will occasionally be a source of deep concern and worry, and these natives may have to assume the care, upbringing and responsibility for a sibling's children. Romance is likely to be with someone in a May-December relationship, either much older or younger, or a mature, conscientious and hardworking person in business, politics or city government. At some period in life, these natives may have to decide between two romantic partners.

Saturn, Ruler of the Ascendant, in the Sixth House in Gemini: You don't mind working hard at your place of employment as long as co-workers and bosses leave you alone. Constant interruptions disturb your train of thought when you are doing paperwork, which could result in costly errors. You prefer a routine type of working condition, doing the same procedure over and over again, as it helps you establish a basic pattern for greater efficiency. It is very upsetting to you when bosses begin to introduce new machinery, techniques or methods of doing things just when you have established a workable method that suits you just fine. You have a powerful analytical mind that tends to make you more serious than the average person. This placement is often referred to as having "an old head on young shoulders." Where health is concerned you will have to develop a positive approach to avoid mental depression that may crop up from time to time. Whenever health problems confront you, see a physician immediately; don't dwell on it mentally and expand the illness out of proportion. The mind is a powerful thing and can create the very illness that you have been brooding about. Your health should be pretty stable and about the only concern may be in later years when you are confronted with bursitis of the shoulders or arthritis of the hands. The health and welfare of siblings, parents, aunts or uncles may instill a sense of responsibility for their care during the latter part of your life.

Saturn, Ruler of the Ascendant, in the Sixth House in Cancer: Saturn in the sixth house of physical health may result in a chronic ailment or a genetic health problem through one of the parents. This is also a placement for those who work for the family establishment or long to have a business they can operate form the home base. These natives are sensitive to criticism when it concerns the way they handle their work-related tasks, and any threat of layoff can throw them into an emotional imbalance as their sense of security is threatened. At some period in life they are likely to hold a supervisory position, which they prefer because they do not appreciate taking orders. They know what duties are expected of them and they handle their tasks in a well-organized, precise manner. Sometimes it may be necessary to work the evening or night shift. These individuals like to make lists of what has to be done during the course of the day and feel they are personally accomplishing something as they cross off completed tasks. They shouldn't expect great achievement or advancement in their professional life; however, they do learn to handle a lot of details, practical techniques and other important items related to the chosen profession that otherwise might have been overlooked. There is greater job efficiency once they have learned to combine sharper skills, refocused their energies and gained a high degree of specialization. In turn, these new skills stimulate major new career opportunities. They should be able to refine and develop their personal talents in a practical way that provides a service to the people around them and to the society in which they live. If a pet is added for maternal purposes, it may entail more responsibility than anticipated.

Saturn, Ruler of the Ascendant, in the Seventh House in Cancer: Saturn in the seventh house does not necessarily deny marriage; however it can delay it as the natives may not seek partners until they are in a position to provide a home and security. Sometimes there is a May-December relationship with someone much older or younger, and others may seek partners who are hard workers, conscientious, conventional and practical. Natives with this placement have to be careful not to shove all responsibilities onto the partner as later in the marriage the partner builds up resentment at having to be the decision maker for both parties. The wise individuals with Saturn in the seventh house make a strong effort to share mutual responsibilities. As the seventh is also a social house, these natives may not prefer social functions or may indicate a preference for just a few close friends or family members. If Saturn receives hard aspects, the mate's parent may disapprove of a child's choice of marriage partner. Others may have to carry the burden for care or responsibility of one of the mate's parents. Business partnerships should be avoided as these individuals can be ruined by treachery in contracts or litigations. A well-aspected Saturn gives a sincere, prudent and faithful marriage or business partner. While marriage partners are not overly demonstrative or emotional, they are trustworthy and honorable in their affections.

Saturn, Ruler of the Ascendant, in the Eighth House in Leo: These natives have an intensified capacity for mental endurance, persistence and concentration that enables them to cope with such things as concerns involving children and financial worries and restrictions. They have a great sense of authority and strength of character and are extremely protective of close family members and especially their children. These natives are likely to attain a position of command and authority after age forty, which suits them far better than a subordinate position. They may have to assume responsibility for other people's resources, even if they prefer not to, because these individuals seem so dependable that others feel they can trust them with their money. With Saturn's placement in Leo, they prefer quality in whatever they purchase, and if they cannot buy the best, then the second best will have to do. The birth and financial welfare of children may be a source of concern. Sexual inhibition can result through rejection of the romantic partner, which in turn has the tendency to deflate the ego and pride in sexual prowess. To cover up their lack of self-confidence in sexual matters, these natives may joke or brag a good deal about their sexual ability.

Saturn, Ruler of the Ascendant, in the Eighth House in Virgo: Saturn in Virgo in the eighth house is more discriminating in its selection of sexual partners. These individuals look first to the partner's manner of dress and behavior pattern, and obscene language and sexual harassment is against their grain. The sexual partner, first of all, has to be clean, well-groomed and tactful in speech and mannerisms. Seldom will these natives have a multitude of partners as fear of sexual diseases keeps them monogamous. However, there is the possibility of sexual indiscretion with a coworker, while others may have strong convictions against such activities. This is a good placement for those who work in the medical or surgical field, work with mutual funds, in banking or city or company payroll and investments.

Saturn, Ruler of the Ascendant, in the Ninth House in Virgo: People with Saturn in Virgo in the ninth house will have to be careful of what they eat and unfamiliar water they drink while traveling in different states or countries to avoid gastric upsets or food poisoning. These individuals are strong believers that a college education is the prime factor in professional success. This is a good placement for those who undertake scientific studies, history, political science or real estate. Travel is usually tied in with work demands or attending seminars that will enhance or introduce new work methods. It is not uncommon for some to travel to distant states or countries for health care treatments. In-laws are likely to be reserved, cold, detached, critical and faultfinding, and it will not be until later in life that they appreciate what the native has contributed to the family. There is also the possibility of caring or taking responsibility for a grandchild. Legal issues are likely to involve accidents or illnesses that may occur through the place of employment.

Saturn, Ruler of the Ascendant, in the Ninth House in Libra: As the ninth house governs the second marriage partner, those seeking a second mate may be looking for one that is reliable, responsible, trustworthy and won't be involved in indiscreet romantic affairs. They may also marry someone older or younger, in a May-December relationship, who is likely to be influential, have a college degree or be in a high ranking position. These natives are not especially emotional or demonstrative, but gentle and tender, and do not believe in an open display of affection. This is an excellent placement for creative writers, teachers, lecturers, diplomats and lawyers or those employed in courts of law.

Saturn, Ruler of the Ascendant, in the Tenth House in Scorpio: There is emphasis on paying one's dues, especially in terms of work and professional matters. Restrictive circumstances keep their noses to the grindstone, forcing them to concentrate on basic responsibilities rather than on the more creative or personally rewarding activities they might prefer. People at work will turn to them for help because of their personal abilities and expertise, and these natives have the know-how they require and can use their skills to improve everyone's situation, including their own. By demonstrating their willingness to take on the difficult assignments and new challenges, they can establish an unquestioned reputation for themselves for getting the job done. Success is not immediate, but comes through persistence and cleverness after many difficulties and obstacles. This placement produces a character that is masterful, subtle and secretive, and it is important for these natives to maintain a good reputation and avoid underhanded tactics; otherwise Saturn can bring them down to their knees through loss of reputation and becoming unpopular through scandal and character assassination. Former President Nixon had Saturn in his natal tenth house and the Watergate scandal cost him America's highest position. These people are likely to work with the lottery, payroll, research or astrology or as detectives or in any vocation that requires deep research, probing and investigation, such as the medical field.

Saturn, Ruler of the Ascendant, in the Eleventh House in Scorpio: Saturn's placement in the eleventh house is one that signifies a loner or one who prefers a few choice friends for social gatherings. These natives don't particularly like to join clubs and organizations because in due time it seems that others want to put them in charge of something; but too many responsibilities cause resentment and the natives eventually quit. Due to Saturn's placement in Scorpio, there will always be one individual, at some period in life, who will try to control these people. If they are gifted with certain talents, it is possible that their intentions are to take unfair advantage of the natives' expertise. Sometimes there is loss or sorrow through friends who either die or move to a distant state and are never seen again. They are extremely loyal to their friends and expect the same in return. When confiding personal secrets to friends who betray them by relaying the information to others, the friends are immediately cut off. I have a client with Saturn in Scorpio in the eleventh house trine the Moon in the eighth house and she inherited (Scorpio) a large sum from an old (Saturn) friend. Saturn has strong occult tendencies in Scorpio, so this is a good placement for those who want to do serious scientific or astrological research or teach the subject.

Saturn, Ruler of the Ascendant, in the Eleventh House in Sagittarius: Saturn in Sagittarius is more tolerant than when placed in Scorpio. There is less intensity in close relationships. There may be many acquaintances, but only a few people who are called friends, and these natives are likely to keep in touch with friends made in school. Teaching or writing profound subjects during the later years of life are great possibilities, especially if the mateiral contains scientific, occult or astrological subjects. Travel to attend seminars or conventions in distant places is also likely. These natives have great enthusiasm, which is contagious as they impart knowledge to others, and by working with people who share their goals and ideals and contributing to the fruits of their own experience, these people can simultaneously broaden their own horizons and aid in the advancement of others. At times, these natives find themselves playing the parental role to friends; on occasion they may bring some degree of obligation or liability into the relationship. It is necessary for them to take the long view of affairs concerning hopes and wishes and not expect quick developments; otherwise the sense of disappointment and frustration is very strong. Due to their professional standing in the business world, they may have to be discriminating in their choice of friends as some may attempt to take unfair advantage of their expertise and profound knowledge or skills.

Saturn, Ruler of the Ascendant, in the Twelfth House in Sagittarius: Saturn placed in the twelfth house can be easily led or influenced by unscrupulous people. Being too trusting of others can be liability. People of different nationalities or backgrounds may at times appear to be working behind their backs or undermining their reputations. Older people, an authoritative figure or in-laws can create psychologically or emotionally upsetting events in their lives.

Saturn, Ruler of the Ascendant, in the Twelfth House in Capricorn: These natives find it difficult to express themselves in large circles of people. They are apt to become involved in isolated pursuits or small, intimate gatherings rather than large groups. On occasion, they may be pushed behind the scenes by actual events occurring in their lives. They can accomplish much if they concentrate their efforts on constructive investigations, research and studies. Now and then they discover that people who enter their lives are not in their best interests, but they may not always know who they are. One particular person who may be older, perhaps a parent or someone of Capricorn coloring (one who has Capricorn Sun or Moon) may upset or irritate these natives almost beyond endurance, causing them to withdraw and seek seclusion. They can accomplish great things working alone in a quiet, isolated state, away from irritating interruptions. The evening or night hours are likely to be their most productive, and the nature is reserved, preferring to work unobserved, alone in secrecy.

Aquarius Ascendant

Fixed Air
Positive Ruler: Uranus

Aquarius is a Uranus-ruled sign of the nature of the eleventh house, the house of the unexpected, unique, different, friends, step-children, daughters- and sons-in-law and clubs or organizations. For this reason, it is natural for Aquarians to be connected with large groups of people, to feel comfortable with computers or other technical equipment.

Character Traits

Aquarius represents high ideals and inventive abilities, individuals who march to the beat of their own drummer. They are generally advanced in thought and ideas. Being of a fixed nature, they stick to their own theories even when others consider them a little eccentric or bizarre. Personal freedom and independence is very important to the Aquarian. These natives cannot be bossed or pushed into action by another. In fact, their love of personal freedom and independence is so important that they have been known to reject relationships that threaten to inhibit their freedom. They are not afraid to try new, different or unusual things, and this may be why more famous people are born under Aquarius. Boris Karloff, the well-known villain of horror films, had his own unique style of acting which made him a legend in the film industry. Aquarius, being air, tries to understand life through people watching, observing their actions to determine their behavior patterns. They are original and inventive and often will be the first ones to develop new and unusual ideas or theories. Few people are aware that Aquarians are goal-oriented individuals. Their goals are usually idealistic and may be concerned with mankind. The main characteristics of Aquarius are generosity, friendliness and love of independence. They are the humani-

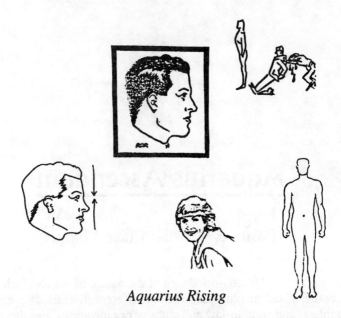

Aquarius Rising

tarians, always seeking to better mankind, seldom prejudiced and able to get along with people from all walks of life. The Aquarian outlook is optimistic, their eyes aimed toward the future, ever ready to make new changes when necessary, never tied to convention and past traditions like Capricorn. Research, discoveries or theories are seldom kept a secret; instead they are passed along to others. Their high degree of intelligence makes them suitable for teaching, research, science, inventing, lecturing, writing, technical fields, music, composing, TV or radio announcing and journalism, with a strong interest in the occult and astrological studies.

Physical Appearance

Individuals will possess some Aquarius qualities and physical features if they have any of the following configurations in the natal chart:
- Aquarius Ascendant
- Uranus in the first house (noticeably stronger if conjunct the Ascendant)
- Uranus within orb of aspect with the Ascendant's degree
- Ruler of the first house (other than Uranus) in Aquarius
- Ruler of the first house conjunct or otherwise in close aspect with Uranus
- Sun or Moon in Aquarius
- Sun or Moon in close aspect with Uranus

- Aquarius intercepted in the first house

Aquarius rising individuals possess one or more of the following features:
- Average height with an upright, erect carriage
- Forehead, nose and mouth being drawn with definite angular lines
- Delicate, clear or pale complexion
- Robust, healthy appearance, even when ill
- Nose often turned up at the tip
- Rectangular or square figure, but strong and well-formed
- Tendency to stoutness in middle age
- Straight up and down profile
- May have unusual eyes; sometimes one is blue and the other brown.

Mentality

Clue Words: Stubborn, witty, curious, intellectual

They dislike underhanded tactics, believing in honesty and fair play. Frank and outspoken in speech, there is much originality in the mental aptitude and they are fixed in their opinions but reasonable, changing their ideas or viewpoints if the new theory appears sounder and is proven to be better. They can be talkative and at other times quiet, and love to debate, taking up the opposite viewpoint just to stir up a good conversation. They possess great magnetic charm, personality and sincerity, and a well-controlled nature with refined sympathies.

Romantic Inclinations

Clue Words: Loyal, curious, loveable, friendly

Aquarius individuals are friendly, easygoing and vivacious. There are times with the opposite sex when Aquarian body language indicates something more than just friendliness and therein lies the problem, especially if the Aquarian is married. Thy are attracted to romantic partners who are intellectual, can hold a good conversation and are wiling to do crazy things on the spur of the moment.

Health

Illness often develops suddenly and unexpectedly, and some may not be curable but will be held in check with medication. In some cases, unique treatments may be necessary such as x-ray, hypnotism, laser, nuclear medicine or electric shock. They have to be careful not to sit on hard chairs for a prolonged period as "charley horses" (cramps) can develop in the calf area. Aquarius and Uranus rule abortions, miscarriages, nervous spasms or twitches, sudden nervous breakdowns, accidents, paralysis, polio, spasmodic pains and problems with the ankle or circulatory system.

Ascendant Ruler in Signs and Houses

Uranus, Ruler of the Ascendant, in the First house in Aquarius: As this is also the ruling planet, there is double emphasis placed on the desire for personal independence. Eccentric habits and beliefs have them going to the beat of their own drummer, and it is difficult for them to conform to conventional standards and procedures. Inventiveness, originality, ingenuity and thoroughness combine with strong intuition and imagination to make very resourceful and industrious individuals. These natives often feel as though they are far more advanced than those around them. Family members may consider them odd or the "black sheep" of the clan. Life during the early years is no doubt quite hectic with many ups and down and sudden changes. A parent may die early in life or the child is separated from a parent due to unusual circumstance. Friends or organized activities become important to these natives as they mature. Accidents or an illness that is difficult to cure are possible if Uranus receives hard aspects, especially from personal planets (Sun, Moon, Mercury, Venus or Mars). Their desire and actions are geared to strike out in new directions and change the familiar patterns of life, but should be done with common sense.

Uranus, Ruler of the Ascendant, in the First House in Pisces: There is a strange pull between a desire to be with large groups and a profound need for isolation. These natives have the ability to detach themselves while at parties or in large groups if they have no interest in the subject matter; they can mentally project themselves elsewhere or, in their mind's eye, plan how they will complete a project they are in the midst of at home or work. There is the tendency to be too trusting and gullible to the point where others often take unfair advantage of them. Hospitals, institutions or jails will touch their lives during their formative years; a parent may be confined, depending on the aspects to Uranus. Sometimes this placement produces a parent who is chronically ill and requires medication to control a health condition. Others may suffer through a parent who is a substance abuser. These natives are extremely sensitive to their surroundings and for this reason should be very careful in their choice of companions. A friend who constantly complains about illness or life's sorrows will eventually permeate the native's emotional and psychological conditioning. Their psychic or intuitive ability often leads them to the study of the occult or astrological subjects.

Uranus, Ruler of the Ascendant, in the First House in Aries: There is more of a desire for freedom and independence than in the first two placements. This gives an active, positive nature that generally surfaces in an independent or unconventional direction. The natives are more apt to be blunt and outspoken in speech, coming right to the point with the truth regardless of whether it hurts the other person's feelings. Possible accidents are also more pronounced as they tend to leap into action without proper forethought for what the situation entails. Injuries to the head or eyes, headaches, sinus conditions and surgery are likely. There is possible separation from a parent, which spurs these natives to become self-contained without benefit of proper parental influence. Whatever field of occupation these natives enter, it will have to be one in which they have complete freedom in decision making. Self-employment is good as they can work independently and at their own pace. They should avoid going into partnership because they eventually balk whenever a partner tries to tell them what to do or tries to make changes that do not appeal to them. Teaching, writing or the study and research of astrology will be undertaken at some period in life.

Uranus, Ruler of the Ascendant in the Second House in Aries: Quick to grasp new opportunities that may lead to new and original ways of gaining money, they can expect fluctuation in finances with abrupt changes in personal finances, bringing periods of plenty followed by periods of lean. Those who are self-employed often have this placement along with those who work on a commission basis. As the second house determines how money is earned, there is an affinity for unique occupations and employment of all kinds. There is possible gain or loss through inventions, mechanical products, astrology, extraordinary skills and electrical things such as computers or video or audio equipment. This placement requires an occupation in which the natives control their own business or earning potential as they do not appreciate others telling them how to spend their money. Adding to a regular savings account is imperative to avoid living in a state of constant uncertainty.

Uranus, Ruler of the Ascendant, in the Second House in Taurus: This is a double configuration of financial gain and loss as personal income is subject to fluctuation. However, due to the fixity of Taurus, there is more determination to hold on to what they have accumulated, financially and materially. They are more likely to set aside funds for protection against upsetting financial upheavals, and there are good intuitive powers which aid in surprising financial gains. Their patience and determination is a constructive plus in whatever field of occupation they choose, especially those involved with earth, money or beautiful products such as land development, home building, framing, horticulture, hair styling, flowers, banking and investments. An unusual and inventive mind is not influenced by the opinions of others, and they are always investigating new and usual fields of interest. Sudden comings and goings and unexpected short travels are the norm. They seek friendships associated with groups and mental stimulation, and have an interest in astrology, radio and TV. They may be accident prone.

Uranus, Ruler of the Ascendant, in the Third House in Taurus: This placement gives determination of steel and great energy for honest, constructive work. These individuals can be quite headstrong with a witty sense of humor, and their intuitive powers are great and often help them to obtain or do things that could not be achieved through ordinary reasoning powers. This placement gives original ideas geared toward new and unique ways of monetary gain, and the mail is likely to contain money and arrive in spurts through advertising or providing unique services. Writing, teaching, books, short travel, lectures and seminars can produce opportunities for financial gain. They may handle finances for a group, club or organization as would be the case with a financial secretary. A brother or sister may experience fluctuating circumstances in the area of finances and at times the native may have to unexpectedly assist with finances. The throat area may be cause for concern and they should guard against throat infections and talking while eating to avoid bits of food suddenly becoming lodged in the throat, creating a choking sensation.

Uranus, Ruler of the Ascendant, in the Fourth House in Taurus: Uranus in the fourth house can influence the lives of natives in the least expected manner. It may disrupt even the most carefully laid plans in practically an instant and conversely fill their lives with eventful activity at times when they have few plans. When these occurrences happen, it may seem that currents are carrying them in the opposite direction from where they intended to go, but they will take the natives to newer destinations which will become much more suitable for home life. There is the possibility of financial gain or drain though a parent. Individuals who have this placement either have extra income from a small business they operate from home or they sell real estate or furniture or work in the building trades, all of which have a tendency to cause personal earnings to fluctuate. There is a great need to own a home for personal security—not a castle, but a comfortable home in which they can escape from the trials and tribulations of the outside world. There is love of peace and harmony, yet the natives find it difficult to achieve these quiet surroundings as friends or relatives repeatedly drop in at a moment's notice.

Uranus, Ruler of the Ascendant, in the Fourth House in Gemini: These natives can rise to the heights in later life if they make a conscious effort to harness the tendency to scatter their mental energies. There is the ability to grasp things quickly and logically, but unless they make a concentrated effort to master one subject, they are likely to scatter their forces and become master of none. This placement is often connected with those in vocations that require a great deal of paperwork, study or correspondence from the home, such as teachers, physicians and insurance agents. There is usually a typewriter, computer, file cabinets, copy machine or fax machine in the home. The Gemini dual sign also indicates two of an item in the home—possibly two TV sets, two computers, two telephones, two refrigerators and so forth. Mental activities—teaching, writing and studies—can become a profitable sideline. There are many changes in the home life during the early years; generally, the natives are viewed by their families as outcasts, different or simply do not understand them. Love of personal freedom and independence may urge these natives to move out of the parent's home at a legal age as they find parents and home life rather restrictive. They may try inventive touches in home decor or turn their ordinary environment to purposes quite different from those for which they are ordinarily used. Family ties are apt to undergo sharp new arrangements that at first seem to jolt the natives into accepting them gracefully, but later are seen as a better way.

Uranus, Ruler of the Ascendant, in the Fifth House in Gemini: The dualistic nature of Gemini can bring many strange love affairs and at times even love at first sight. The unexpected nature of Uranus can bring sudden love relationships which just as suddenly end. There is a tendency toward unconventional or impulsive love affairs, sometimes with a neighbor or school chum. This is a great placement for teachers who work with autistic children or those who are borderline geniuses, and for those who have a dramatic flair in writing or announcing on radio or TV. As the fifth house is also the house of creativity, writing ability may be present; if so, these natives should make it a point to write short stories, articles or plays. They can become quite impatient and lose interest if attempting to write novels or long, drawn out textbooks. They may have to take care of a sibling's child due to unexpected circumstances, and their own children could be a source of mental anxiety and worry.

Uranus, Ruler of the Ascendant, in the Fifth House in Cancer: These natives are very sensitive and their feelings are easily hurt, especially in the area of romance. They have a psychological fear of rejection and when a date has to cancel an evening engagement they take it personally and feel the date never wanted to go out with them in the first place. Their feelings and emotions are subject to constant upheaval, which makes these natives appear unstable or peculiar to others. Although these natives love the home and children, they go through periodic upsetting conditions and changes. They never really come to grips with family and children, and there is the possibility of unexpected separation or loss through the affairs of children.

Uranus, Ruler of the Ascendant, in the Sixth House in Cancer: Fear of insecurity can throw these natives into an emotional mess when there is a threat or rumor of a layoff at work. These sudden and unexpected changes in the job situation can affect their health. As an added defense against future employment upheavals, some may try their hand at freelancing or another sideline occupation that can be operated from the home. They work well in occupations dealing with the general public and often feel the need to create excitement at work when duties become excessively boring. These natives may be subjected to sudden illness or accidents, and a family member or an aunt or uncle may develop an illness that requires specialized treatment such as lasers, x-rays or nuclear medicine. They may work with a friend or a friend may be constructive in helping them find employment. Work hours usually fluctuate or there may be unusual jobs, skills or equipment they learn to operate such as computers, x-ray equipment, copy or fax machines, or video and audio equipment. Also possible is an affiliation with radio, TV or other far-reaching media in which public contacts play a role in their occupational duties. Regarding health, Uranus seems to act largely through the nerves, the mind and emotional instability when positioned in Cancer. It produces more value in later life through the vitalizing power it projects, and inclines to the newer and more unconventional modes of medical treatment such as electricity, hypnotism and radiation. If Uranus receives hard aspects in the sixth house in Cancer, sometimes an illness or disease is genetic, deep-seated, complicated and often incurable. With soft aspects to Uranus, these very different and unique treatments may be the ones necessary, not for a cure, but for holding the disease in remission.

Uranus, Ruler of the Ascendant, in the Sixth House in Leo: The influence is similar to the above paragraph except that health problems may pertain to unusual back problems (protruding tail bone), pinched nerves in the lower back or unusual eye problems that cannot be cured but can be corrected through laser treatments or wearing eyeglasses with unusual prescriptions. Women who have hard aspects to Uranus in Leo in the sixth house may experience unusual difficulty in childbirth or may be unable to conceive due to an unusual formation of the reproductive system. Regarding working conditions, there is a greater need for personal freedom in decision making and a strong desire to hold a supervisory or management position.

Uranus, Ruler of the Ascendant, in the Seventh House in Leo: It's difficult to be involved with another person on any level and not have to alter, at least slightly, one's daily routine. Yet in the ideal relationship, limits on personal freedom are a tradeoff—giving up some individuality in order to gain the greater benefits that can be found in joint efforts. These natives are likely to be attracted to mates or business partners who possess unusual, inventive or creative ideas. Their unique sense of humor and uncommon taste in food, style of dress and entertainment is probably what draws these natives to them in the first place. Yet at times they may balk at the partner's need for personal freedom and wanting to spend considerable time with friends and associates in social functions—without the Aquarius rising individual. Uranus can bring sudden breaks, crises and disturbances where mutual endeavors are concerned, including possible trouble through unconventional alliances or unwise romances with partners who may be married. It can bring temporary fascination with the opposite sex, rather than true love. In a male's chart the wife may have unusual problems with childbirth or during pregnancy.

Uranus, Ruler of the Ascendant, in the Seventh House in Virgo: This influence is similar to the above paragraph except there may be an attraction to those of a lower status or an unconventional relationship with someone encountered through a work-related situation. The marriage partner may be involved with politics or employed by the city as a police officer, firefighter, etc. The sympathy is easily turned to antipathy, and tolerance to a hasty and critical intolerance of mates or close associates.

Uranus, Ruler of the Ascendant, in the Eighth House in Virgo: The mind is subtle, independent and original. These natives are quiet, fond of curiosities and science, and likely to possess an unusual or witty sense of humor. This placement makes a good mechanic, someone who seems to have a natural talent for working with tools, chemistry, electronics or electricity. The unexpected usually occurs at work in which accidents or an illness may require a lengthy recuperation and possibly collecting sick benefits or Worker's Compensation. These individuals can be obstinate and eccentric, but normally inoffensive unless someone intrudes on their privacy.

Uranus, Ruler of the Ascendant, in the Eighth House in Libra: These natives are likely to gain through the resources of a marriage partner, and there is possible financial gain or loss through partnerships. The nature is restless, fond of travel, ambitious and quick tempered, and the imagination is good. There is great literary skill as these natives take great pains to research their material before writing. It gives sexual and personal magnetism which may incline the natives to sexual curiosity through unconventional affairs. This is not the best placement for longevity in marriage as there is danger of separation through divorce or death. If Uranus receives hard aspects, the natives would be wise to avoid mutual financial endeavors that involve friends or organized activities. Co-singing a mortgage for or lending money to friends can also have a disturbing effect on the relationship when the money is not repaid or friends are unable to continue making payments on a loan and the natives have to assume payment for the balance.

Uranus, Ruler of the Ascendant, in the Ninth House in Scorpio: This placement gives great strength of mind, will, persistence and determination along with excellent powers of concentration for writing technical books or those on astrology and occult subjects. There is possible gain through royalties from published material. This placement can produce fluctuating circumstances through mutual funds connected with distant matters, legal affairs, religion or teaching, and the natives may have to travel suddenly and unexpectedly to attend funerals for friends in distant cities. The nature is usually quite secretive, stubborn, reserved, aggressive, forceful and rebellious, especially with other people who may try to change their opinions. These natives have the willpower to pursue personal goals and self-advancement. Depending on the aspects to Uranus, a brother- or sister-in-law may be in charge of a parent's will and if there are hard aspects to Uranus, the marriage partner is likely to receive nothing in the way of financial or material gain through the parent's estate. Unusual circumstances surrounding matters of death and legal issues may confront the natives at some point in life. For example, they may be faced with a major decision in which they have to sign a legal document for medical termination of life support for a family member. For others, it may be a formal legal document to have a vicious neighborhood dog put to sleep because it attacked a child or family member. Sometimes there is an obsession with religion, writing a book or deep-rooted racial issues. Often this placement gives original and unusual views and ideas regarding religion and philosophy and a likelihood of breaking away from the orthodox. There are unexpected travels, some with friends and others with group tours or to attend conventions and seminars.

Uranus, Ruler of the Ascendant, in the Tenth House in Sagittarius: This placement indicates much travel in connection with work, and these natives may travel to attend conventions connected with their profession or religious retreats. This is probably one of the best signs and placements for Uranus as it promote the humanitarian spirit and enthusiastic willingness to help others through the career. These individuals are extremely fond of freedom in action and decision making, adventurous, progressive and daring to promote beliefs and undertakings which are not always orthodox or accepted by the general public. Sagittarius offers great protection against enemies and it is a fortunate position that gives inner drive for professional advancement. Teaching, writing, travel, religion and contacts with people from all walks of life will be experienced through the occupation. As Sagittarius is a mutable sign, these natives are likely to wear many different "hats," sometimes spreading themselves too thin when they take on more projects than they can adequately handle. They have to guard against this tendency as a high degree of continued nervous stress can affect the health. Originality is a marked feature as they encounter strange and eventful circumstances through the profession. They do better professionally if they are self-employed as they tend to overthrow all bonds of restriction and limitation. Because there is such a strong dislike of routine work, these natives work best independently and enjoy careers in which they can dress as they please and work at their own pace at whatever hours they please. Sometimes this is indicative of two simultaneous occupations, one full time and the other a part-time sideline. Teachers, novelists, reporters, publishers, astrologers, flight attendants are likely to have this placement.

Uranus, Ruler of the Ascendant, in the Eleventh House in Sagittarius: The influence is similar to the previous paragraph except the humanitarian efforts are likely to be geared toward organizations connected with community service. Uranus is another of those planets that gives a wide diversity in age so it is not uncommon for natives with this placement to enjoy friendships with those of vastly different ages and those who are of a different cultural background, race, color or creed. Friends are likely to be made while attending conferences, traveling or on group tours, and this placement brings unusual people into the life, some of whom may be eccentric, adventurers, astrologers, inventors, geniuses, writers or government executives or politicians. As the eleventh house is the opposite of the fifth, these natives may encounter unusual friends who may slowly develop into lovers. Unexpected legal matters may involve affairs of step-children, friends, clubs and organizations or a daughter- or son-in-law.

Uranus, Ruler of the Ascendant, in the Eleventh House in Capricorn: This placement gives stability in reasoning and generally a profound, penetrating mind. It intensifies the ambitions, perseverance and independence, and their goals may be centered around unique and original undertakings. This is a good placement for those who want to enter the professional side of astrology and earn a living through writing or teaching occult or astrological subjects. Friends are likely to be older professionals who may work in municipal offices or be in positions of power, trust and responsibility. These natives are likely to hold executive positions with clubs or organizations, and have many acquaintance but only a few regarded as true, close friends.

Uranus, Ruler of the Ascendant, in the Twelfth House in Capricorn: Unforeseen circumstances or situations may restrict these natives from forming close ties with friends or taking an active role in a club or organization. It may be a job or caring for an older family member that turns these natives into loners, creating a sort of isolated condition. Sometimes there is separation or abandonment through one of the parents. This placement can produce sudden and unexpected illnesses that sometimes turn into chronic conditions. These natives must always be careful of the bony structure of the body and try to prevent falls that could result in broken bones. For those who are active with clubs or organizations, there may be times when they are likely to feel as though their hard work and volunteer efforts are going unnoticed and unappreciated. After a while, they may lessen involvement in these activities and take a passive role. They have to be especially watchful of acquaintances who put on airs and pretend to be more than what they really are in an attempt to gain the natives' confidence. Professional individuals, politicians and old friends in the business world may attempt to steer them in the wrong direction, and they have to be very selective when inviting others into their social circle as some may attempt to undermine their reputation or credibility out of jealousy for what the natives have accomplished. The temptation for a clandestine affair should be avoided because it is likely to involve someone older, a professional person or someone married; emotional and psychological hurt will result when it ends.

Pisces Ascendant

Mutable   Water
Passive   Ruler: Neptune

Pisces is a Neptune-ruled sign of the nature of the twelfth house, the house of secrets, confinement, intuition and creativity. For this reason it is natural for natives with Pisces on the Ascendant to experience a secret sorrow, to have something to do with individuals who may be mentally, emotionally or physically handicapped and feel a need from time to time for periods of quiet solitude and isolation.

Character Traits

Pisces is a water sign and relates to the subconscious mind. The main characteristics of Pisces are gentleness and compassion with a retiring nature. The two fishes connected by a cord and swimming in opposite directions clearly indicate the pull in the dualistic nature of Pisces natives.

They can be at a party and mingle with friends, and then suddenly feel bored and mentally detach themselves, becoming buried in deep, reflective thoughts. They have to guard against unscrupulous people who may try to manipulate or take unfair advantage of their kindness and generosity. Their sympathetic nature often turns into a form of martyrdom to where they may give the shirts off their backs, if necessary; but if their generosity is not appreciated, they can become deeply hurt and nurse this hurt into a state of depression.

Many of them are endowed with artistic or musical ability, and the need for self-expression and interpretation of emotions often leads them into acting carers. The imaginative mind produces many poets, playwrights and authors, especially of detective stories. The need for meditation or solitude coupled with the love of working with masses of people helps Pisces find inner peace within the walls of a monastery, nunnery, hospital or other large institution such as a nursing home or prison.

They are easygoing individuals but not overly industrious. Changeable, moody and temperamental, they can be talkative once they get started but can also be quite secretive and silent. They are sometimes difficult to know and this may be due to the fact that they are often taken advantage of and their generosity is abused to the point where they become loners. Sometimes they lead double lives or experience secret sorrows.

These individuals have quick, comprehensive, intelligent minds with good judgment and the ability to do many things. They may be overly fond of alcoholic beverages or the opposite—overly sensitive and unable to tolerate them. Others may be sensitive to certain foods or medication. Some have musical or artistic talents, and they are fond of the good things in life and inclined to be overly self-indulgent. Some have the tendency for clairvoyance or psychic ability. They are romantic and sentimental, although they can go to the extreme and be cold. Very impressionable, they are thrown completely off balance by confusion, excessive noise and chaos. Losses through false friends or secret enemies may trouble them from time to time.

Physical Appearance

Individuals posses some Pisces qualities and physical features if they have any of the following configurations in the natal chart:
- Pisces rising
- Neptune in the first house (noticeably stronger if conjunct the Ascendant)
- Neptune within orb of the Ascendant's degree
- Ruler of the first house in Pisces
- Ruler of the first house conjunct or otherwise in close aspect with Neptune
- Sun or Moon in Pisces
- Sun or Moon in close aspect with Neptune
- Pisces intercepted in the first house

Pisces rising individuals possess one or more of the following features:
- Nose joins the brow with very little indentation, being parallel with forehead line
- Often has droopy eyelids on the side, similar to actress Debbie Reynolds
- Eyes may protrude from the sockets with heavy upper lids

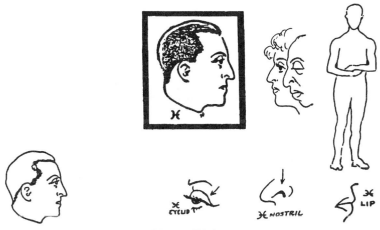

Pisces Rising

- Dropping lines at the corners of the mouth
- Nostrils often turned up as if pulled up with a cord
- Pale complexion; eyes may have dreamy look
- Often holds head down when walking, as though looking for something
- Medium height, but can become stout with age due to water retention
- Short fin-like limbs, small hands and feet, awkward walk

Mentality

Clue Words: Emotional, sensitive, psychic, mediumistic

Music is very calming to the nervous system, and they have strong intuitive or psychic ability. Some have musical, artistic or writing talent. They care very little for details as they see the oneness of life. Mentally, they desire to be free form every restriction, but are usually restricted by family, a health condition or the environment. Every time these natives free themselves from one situation, they seem to immediately tie themselves to another. Emotional in nature, they love freedom and laughter, although they can cry just as quickly, and sometimes laugh and cry at almost the same time. Their psychic powers help them see the past and the future, and they seem to know that the present is not everything and that however beautiful existing things are at the moment, some day they will be destroyed. Although they mentally love social occasions and pleasure, they will on occasion slip away and let guests entertain themselves. They are seldom on time, and are easily moved by patriotic themes or the suffering of others.

Romantic Inclinations

Clue Words: Receptive, emotional, passionate, protective, tender, affectionate

Pisces can be one of the most passionate and gentle of all signs. The emotions carry these natives to the very heights of experience and, coupled with the ability to show their affection, tenderness and considerable love, can be the rarest of lovers. They are very protective and never make sexual demands if the mate is not feeling up to par.

Health

The most vulnerable area for Pisces natives is their strong imagination, which can produce illnesses of a psychosomatic nature. They should protect themselves against stress that could lead to nervous or mental breakdowns or disorders. There is also the tendency to be ultra-sensitive to certain medication or food, and they should purchase well-made shoes to avoid foot trouble. There may be a weak vitality subject to illnesses that are difficult to diagnose, and for this reason they should always seek a second medical opinion before agreeing to surgery or unusual treatments.

Ascendant Ruler in the Signs and Houses

Neptune, Ruler of the Ascendant, in the First House in Pisces: Whenever a planet is in its own sign and also ruler of the Ascendant, there is a double emphasis on the character traits. These natives are more apt to be psychically sensitive to their environment, surroundings and people with whom they associate. For this reason they must choose their companions wisely. Having friends who are constant complainers about health, working conditions or marital status will eventually rub off on the natives, who tend to absorb these negative suggestions and thoughts. There is a sort of quiet dignity to the nature, one that is serious, profound and contemplative. This placement intensifies mediumistic qualities and gives them the ability to detect when someone is being deceptive or trying to pull something over on them. There may be some kind of disability or illness that requires medication to control, and there is a greater chance for sensitivity to certain medication or food products. Substance abuse, whether alcohol, tobacco or illicit drugs, should be avoided at all costs since Pisces natives are very susceptible and easily fall under their influence. There will always be an air or secrecy surrounding their internal affairs, which makes it extremely difficult for others to know whether they stand with them. This placement attracts peculiar people, psychics, artists, musicians, chemists and also takes them into strange and mysterious places. There is a love of peace and harmony, but they can be assertive when they feel someone is taking unfair advantage of them or of another individual. There will be times when an air of uncertainty, confusion or deception surrounds circumstances in life or close relationships. A receptivity to psychic conditions can run to the extreme, allowing the feelings to act instead of good, sound judgment. They are likely to come in contact with bars, bartenders, nightclubs, hospitals, boats, water, chemicals and anything that has an odor to it, such as paint, perfume and gasoline. People who are con artists, drug addicts, alcoholics, in the medical field, or emotionally, mentally or physically handicapped will touch on the lives of these natives from time to time.

Neptune, Ruler of the Ascendant, in the First House in Aries: The influence of this placement is similar to the above paragraph except there is an underlying hot temper that can be quite explosive once aroused. These natives are sympathetic, gentle and compassionate but when they see that someone is being mistreated or their patience is being pushed to the extreme, they assert themselves in such a manner that surprises even their closest friends. There is a strong independent streak in their nature; they tolerate being bossed, but only to a certain degree before they retaliate. They are more apt to undergo surgery or suffer from migraine headaches or sinus conditions. Sensitivity to certain drugs, medication or food is likely to react on the face, causing hives or a flushed appearance. There is a greater love of travel, and originality in ideas and concepts regarding various subjects. There may be secret dealings with young men, either of a personal or business nature.

Neptune, Ruler of the Ascendant, in the Second House in Aries: This placement gives a strong desire to make money or obtain possessions easily and quickly; as a result there will be a need to discriminate between what is necessary and what is being purchased on impulse. Otherwise, these natives can get into financial difficulties through lack of proper forethought. They may feel they must have a secret bank account or money hidden from other members of the family. This is not to withhold any great sum from the marriage partner or associate, but because they feel it necessary to put something aside for a special occasion and believe the partner is likely to spend it all. There is a need to handle their own earnings and to be able to make purchases without having to ask another person. Gifts form others are likely to be bottles of wine or liquor, perfume and specialty items that are handmade. These natives want to own a boat or a country home near the water to which they can escape from the hectic turmoil of the outside world. They may earn money through creative enterprises, chemistry, psychology, photography, boating or items in the liquid state.

Neptune, Ruler of the Ascendant, in the Second House in Taurus: Neptune is better situated in Taurus than Aries. This is an excellent placement for hair stylists, bank employees who work in vaults handling secret storage compartments or any field in which music, art or things of beauty are involved. Taurus is an earth sign, so these natives are more apt to desire a quiet country getaway where they can be at one with the universe contemplating the peace and quiet of the lakes, woods and wild animals. They are less likely to purchase items on impulse. Although they would like to make easy money, they take time to investigate an enterprise to determine if there is any monetary risk involved. These natives are more responsive to romantic interludes, love and affection, and as this is a Venus-ruled sign, they have to be careful of being overly generous with loved ones and the opposite sex.

Neptune, Ruler of the Ascendant, in the Third House in Taurus: There is a highly developed capacity for visualization on a practical level. These natives have the ability to plan in their mind's eye what they want to accomplish or create, and then immediately put their ideas into practical use. Intuitive, they may be able to read other people's minds, and are likely to earn money through writing books or articles on occult or astrological subjects. These natives may be slow learners due to the tendency for daydreaming and fantasizing, but once learned the subject is seldom forgotten. Misunderstandings through the written or spoken word and in dealings with siblings may have an effect on financial gain or loss, and travel may be conducive for financial gain. They should use extreme care when signing legal contracts or agreements that may in some way have an effect on personal finances. Some may receive gifts, letters or phone calls form secret admirers. These natives may be faced with situations that require clearly defined goals, and success will not come through immediate results but through gradual effort on a consistent basis, bringing increased clarity of purpose. When they want to make an important decision, they should visualize their thoughts objectively and then follow through on a steady, uninterrupted course.

Neptune, Ruler of the Ascendant, in the Third House in Gemini: This is a mutable planet in a mutable house in a mutable sign. If these natives can harness the tendency to scatter their energies, they can accomplish great feats in writing or the creative arts. They are excellent teachers and transmitters of knowledge, sensing when someone in the audience is getting bored or restless, and then immediately changing to a new line of thought or action. These natives are sociable with a need to communicate and exchange ideas and views. There is a capacity for fine work for draftsmanship or the cultural arts. These natives find it difficult to come up with ideas of their own and do better if they work with someone who can provide the necessary stimuli. At times there will be a great need for mental escapism through deep research, studies, reading or working on the computer or visual or audio equipment. Due to the changeable Gemini nature, they should make a special effort to speak clearly, leaving little chance for complicated misunderstandings and confusion. This placement often produces step-brothers or sisters or their own siblings may have minor handicaps, learning disabilities or speech impediments.

Neptune, Ruler of the Ascendant, in the Fourth House in Gemini: This is another one of those configurations in which half-brothers or sisters are possible. One of the parents may harbor a deep-rooted secret, and sometimes there are peculiar or strange conditions surrounding the home base or through family ties. There is possible gain or loss of property through strange or complicated situations involving wills, document or siblings. There is a greater desire for escapism from the trials and tribulations of the outside world, and some may have two homes—one a hideaway cottage near water or a lake. Others may escape through reading, studying or excessive television watching. The emotions, rather than logic, usually prevail when they are faced with important decisions. This is a good placement for writers, bookkeepers or computer programmers who can work in the quiet, isolated surroundings of home.

Neptune, Ruler of the Ascendant, in the Fourth House in Cancer: These natives are ultra-sensitive to criticism and surrounding conditions. They require light-colored walls and large spacious rooms with large, unshaded windows so they can watch the birds as they eat from the feeder and the wind gently sway the leaves back and forth in the trees. Just a few minutes of contemplating nature's wonders can ease inner tension for these Pisces individuals. Criticism, no matter how constructive it may be, creates deep psychological hurts. Some are likely to eat excessively as a balm to what they feel are injured feelings. A home is a must for these natives, preferably near water or at least with a pond on the property. There is almost always a musical instrument in the home—piano, organ or stereo. They are very patriotic and easily moved to tears on national holidays when the country's flag is flying or "Taps" is being played. There is a strong belief in maintaining traditional holiday rituals such as a family tablecloth and special candles at Christmas or Easter. One of the parents may have had a serious ailment that required medication to keep it under control, and secret arrangements concerning parental property may be a source of gain or loss.

Neptune, Ruler of the Ascendant, in the Fifth House in Leo: Some natives with this placement have always wanted to be clowns entertaining children. It gives them the ability to put on a false face and for a brief moment be something other than what they really are. As romance is covered under the fifth house, some may experience faithlessness or confusion and sorrow in love affairs. They may drink alcoholic beverages excessively either to bolster the ego and self-confidence or because they are with others who drink and they don't want to feel like outsiders. However, it is possible that pleasurable drinking at parties or football games can lead to serious health complications in which the natives end up in the hospital having their stomachs pumped. But as a rule these natives are inclined to have high morals and be kind and generous. They are easily moved by affairs of children and can be overly generous, especially if they are in need of money or if a child is handicapped or has a minor health problem. One particular child is likely to have problems with the feet and may require corrective braces or be extremely sensitive, shy and introverted. In some fields the natives possess creative, artistic or musical talent. Depending on the aspects to Neptune it is not uncommon for some women to harbor a deep-rooted secret concerning a love affair or delivery of a child. With hard aspects to Neptune, children may become substance abusers. In later life the natives may have to take medication for a heart problem or high blood pressure.

Neptune, Ruler of the Ascendant, in the Sixth House in Leo: Although there are strong moral convictions, there is still the possibility of hidden intrigue or a love affair with someone met through a work-related situation. Neptune in the sixth house often creates confusion with medical examinations so a second opinion is strongly suggested, especially where health matters concern the eyes, heart or back. These natives should always wear eye protectors at work if chemicals are involved or when handling items containing dangerous odors and fumes that may affect the eyes. They require peace and quiet in order to function properly in their line of work, and there are times when they find themselves working in an obscure, isolated environment in order to accomplish a difficult creative project. In a female's chart, a complicated pregnancy or delivery of a child may react on the health. An aunt or uncle or other close family relative is likely to suffer severe heart, back or eye problems. Many of these natives use sports, whether watching TV or through active participation, as a pleasurable means of escapism. Others prefer dancing, music, theater, travel, boating, fishing, swimming, taking cruises or going to amusement parks and family picnics as a source of relaxation for the nervous system.

Neptune, Ruler of the Ascendant, in the Sixth House in Virgo: Things and people these natives rely on from day to day seem less dependable than they ordinarily are. There is a slight likelihood these individuals will be misled by someone who performs services on their behalf. To prevent this, a few additional steps should be taken to safeguard valuables and double check all facets of the rendered services to make sure everything is done correctly. They may be somewhat more sensitive to conditions in their environment and receptive to the thoughts and intentions of others. In order to decrease the body's subsequent vulnerability, the imagination needs to be kept in proper perspective to the natives' need to allow for more than the usual precautionary measures to improve the health. This is especially important during the cold and flu season or any period when a virus is making the rounds. They will certainly want to obtain more than one authoritative opinion before deciding on any drastic measures designed to improve their physical well being. Although they are concerned about hygiene, it is dangerous to mix household chemicals together, thinking that several combinations of a cleaning compound will do a far better job. It is possible that at some point these natives may be tempted to combined these cleaning chemicals, creating harmful gaseous odors and creating a suffocating or choking effect for the lungs. It is also advisable to be especially watchful with prescribed medication. When having the pharmacist refill a prescription, these natives should make sure it is exactly what the physician ordered. Whether in a hospital or obtaining a refill, doctors, nurses and pharmacists have been known to make errors. For their protection, the natives should be on guard against such possibilities.

Neptune, Ruler of the Ascendant, in the Seventh House in Virgo: With the ruling planet in the seventh house, these natives have great fantasies and illusions from early childhood about love relationships and the marriage partner. Books or movies such as *Beauty and the Beast*, *Cinderella* or *Snow White* are probably among the favorites, and almost anything that enhances interest in love, romance and marriage. The hope is that these natives do not place these relationships on too high of a pedestal because a rude awakening probably sets in shortly after marriage when they discover the partner's faults and undesirable habits. There are periods in life in which worries and anxieties concerning the health of the marriage partner or a close associate are of primary concern. These natives are very serious in handling what they feel are their responsibilities and this part of their nature enables them to achieve success through hard work and perseverance. But it seems that no matter how much effort they put forth, they may always feel a lack of contentment with what they have achieved, as though the fulfillment of their ambitions has been thwarted. They will have to strive to maintain a positive outlook, no matter how bleak the situation may appear. The marriage or business partner is likely to bring them in contact with police activity and the political or public side of life. The marriage partner may work for the city or in the medical field. Secrets surrounding the affairs of an aunt, uncle, niece or nephew may come to their attention.

Neptune, Ruler of the Ascendant, in the Eighth House in Libra: This is a very creative position for literature and the arts in which the natives can gain financially through royalties or sales thereof. This placement enhances the attractive and sexual side of the nature and tends to work through the emotional and passionate side, which can give a somewhat unorthodox view regarding the choice of sexual partners. There is usually an unexplainable fascination for members of the opposite sex. The result can produce complicated, deceptive or clandestine affairs with married individuals or the native may be married at the time of the indiscretion. As this is the second house of money of the seventh house of partners, it is possible that from time to time they may secretly withhold some of their earnings or monetary gains, such as unforeseen bonuses or winnings through card games or check pools.

Neptune, Ruler of the Ascendant, in the Eighth House in Scorpio: These natives can be extremely creative, yet on a practical and useful level. They may like to refinish, rebuild or renew old homes or furniture. This is a difficult placement for a sensitive planet like Neptune since it is in the secretive house of Scorpio, natural ruler of the eighth house. It can make the native skeptical, sarcastic, critical and faultfinding, wanting everything to be perfect if at all possible. There is likely to be some secrecy, confusion or deception through inheritance, insurance policies or Workers's Compensation. This is a double eighth house and Scorpio combination, which colors the native with a certain degree of secrecy, intensity and strong sensual passions. Neptune can indicate possible loss of financial or material matters through trickery or deception. With soft aspects to Neptune in the eighth house the natives can have strong intuitive or psychic instincts. Sometimes this placement brings disturbing dreams or nightmares.

Neptune, Ruler of the Ascendant, in the Ninth House in Scorpio: There can be strong religious convictions or the very opposite in which the natives go to the extreme in seeking spiritual revelations. I have seen Neptune in the ninth house in Scorpio in the charts of people who relocate to other states to escape the embarrassment of bankruptcy, hoping to begin life anew in a different city, only to discover that opportunities were better where they formerly resided. These people are perfectionists who seek higher education and a professional career through things that they can research and study; they bury themselves in their work, sometimes to the point of ignoring the wants and desires of others and family members. Legal involvement may be centered around insurance settlements, wills or unusual circumstances involving the death of something or someone. There is possible financial or material gain through in-laws, but if Neptune receives hard aspects, an in-law could use trickery to gain through wills, legacies or an inheritance. This is also indicative of complicated issues surrounding divorce settlements involving child support or division of mutual funds and possessions. There is love of travel, especially by water. This placement gives highly inspirational feelings, experiences and prophetic dreams, and is good for those who may want to study the occult, astrology or the medical field. Sometimes they become ill while traveling and are confined in a hospital away from home.

Neptune, Ruler of the Ascendant, in the Ninth House in Sagittarius:
This placement emphasizes the desire for travel and researching new religious concepts, possibly seeking something more spiritual. This is a good placement for Neptune, making it more humanitarian and sincere with ambitions determination. There is ability for farsightedness, prophetic dreams, visions, intuition and inspiration. They have to be careful of food and water when they travel as some may contain an unfamiliar substance that could cause a reaction. This placement can result in Legionnaire's Disease, where people become ill and are hospitalized as the result of food eaten at a convention or seminar. People from all walks of life, color, creed and cultural background touch on the lives of these natives from time to time and some may not be trustworthy or reliable. When they are faced with a jury, it is likely to concern racial, sexual or job discrimination, drug dealers, thieves or convicts who take hostages.

Neptune, Ruler of the Ascendant, in the Tenth House in Sagittarius:
This placement indicates possible danger of deception from others connected with the profession—someone who may attempt to undermine the reputation or standing in the community. People who have this configuration may change or alter their professional or company name or use a pseudonym at some period in their life. They work in the fields of communication, publicity, advertising, chemistry, anesthesia, hospitals, photography, film acting, singing or employment with the city in community hospitals, institutions, reformatories, jails and prisons. Contacts with people who are weird, different, psychic, former inmates, musicians, artists, politicians or in the medical field may be possible through work-related duties. As Neptune governs photography, their photos may appear in the local newspaper. One of the parents may have health problems in the lung area, liver or hips, or require frequent hospital visits. When it comes to travel in connection with work, these

natives should always check their flight tickets to make sure all is in order because confusion can create errors; for example, being forced to remain on standby because an airline employee accidentally omitted the seat number on the ticket.

Neptune, Ruler of the Ascendant, in the Eleventh House in Capricorn: There are practical ambitions and good reasoning power coupled with comprehensive thoroughness that draws these natives into new and unusual lines of professional interest. Hard work and conscientious effort toward a desired goal enables them to reach the heights of success in their chosen fields. This is an excellent placement for real estate, political science, teaching history, the occult and astrology. They may go through a period of depression as a result of deception through what they consider a reliable and trusted friend. Because of their specialized talents, there is always someone who wants to take unfair advantage of their expertise. They do their best inspirational writing or creative arts in an isolated state where they can work alone in quiet solitude without fear of constant interruption from friends and phone calls. They may discover that when confronted with a truly difficult task there is a greater chance of success if they work during the evening hours. It may be difficult at times to truly get close to or understand a daughter- or son-in-law or they may undergo a period of severe depression and confusion. This placement can also produce step-grandchildren, those of a daughter- or son-in-law through a previous marriage.

Neptune, Ruler of the Ascendant, in the Twelfth House in Aquarius: This placement can hold tremendous possibilities for new ideas and concepts. The imaginative mind can expand creatively through music, art, photography or writing. These natives may feel compelled to help those less fortunate or afflicted, something they do through the medical field, volunteering in nursing homes or through the use of psychology and astrology. They are likely to become susceptible to environmental conditions. For this reason they must maintain a positive outlook, both for mental and physical health. Sometimes they may experience allergies or illnesses that are difficult to define or that require medication to keep under control. With Neptune in Aquarius in the twelfth house, they have to be careful in the choice of companions as friends can easily turn into enemies and this may have a disturbing effect on their ability to trust new companions. Sometimes there are hidden matters, behind the scenes activities, confusion and chaotic conditions through clubs and organization that can also have a disturbing emotional and psychological effect. This is an excellent placement for those who work in confining or isolated conditions in which x-ray equipment, lasers, computers or electric typewriters are used. Such would be the case with hospital laboratory work. Creative writers and artists may isolate themselves from the phone and social activities to complete a pet project. There is a greater sense of perception and intuition. These natives have great ability for creativity along new lines of thought that is both unusual and somewhat unconventional. Successful outlets for Neptune in Aquarius in the twelfth house are mediumship, psychic research, psychic healing, detective work, laboratory research, the medical field, hospital or institutional work, photography, bartending and occult or astrological research, studies and investigations.